WHERE THE HELL IS
TUCUMCARI

WHERE THE HELL IS
TUCUMCARI

MARY ANN FROEDE

authorHOUSE®

AuthorHouse™
1663 Liberty Drive
Bloomington, IN 47403
www.authorhouse.com
Phone: 1-800-839-8640

Published by AuthorHouse   03/22/2012

ISBN: 978-1-4685-5867-8 (sc)
ISBN: 978-1-4685-5866-1 (e)

Library of Congress Control Number: 2012903706

Dedicated to Jim and my children, Rick, Ruthi and Steve
who shared our adventure.

O ur car coasted into the driveway. The front door opened and my husband, Jim, danced into the room singing "I've just applied for the position as pastor of the church in Tucumcari, New Mexico." I cried out "Where the hell is Tucumcari?" We both dashed for the atlas maps and a magnifying glass to find a tiny dot in Northern New Mexico, halfway between Albuquerque, New Mexico and Amarillo, Texas. Thus began our great adventure.

By way of explanation, we got to this point in our lives after Jim interrupted his college education by serving as a decorated combat medic in World War II. He had returned home to complete his college work and receive his bachelor of science degree from the University of Wisconsin. We met and then married in August of '49 and he graduated in January of '50. His goal was to be a doctor with an internship at Gorgas Hospital in Panama as a parasitologist. Having to wait to get into medical school, he took a job with a pharmaceutical firm in Milwaukee, where we were living at the time. He was transferred to Sacramento and three years and two children later, we both had a remarkable call to the ministry. Off to San Anselmo, to San Francisco Theological Seminary for Jim to complete his masters in theology. I worked as an office nurse and lab technician at various medical facilities while the children were cared for by babysitters. When Jim and his classmates were ready to graduate, there were bulletin boards with available positions for the "interns". Jim's buddies all ganged up and said "Froede, here's the one for you". It was assistant pastor at Beverly Hills Presbyterian Church. He took the dare and three months later we were on our way to our first job. After three years as assistant there (which is a book in itself), Jim was ready to have his own "domain" . . . thus the move to Tucumcari.

—⟶ɯ⟵—

Before memory fails me or senility sets in and all is replaced by fantasy, I must record the wonderful experiences of my sojourn in the high desert as a young mother. In a town of about 6,000 souls, Tucumcari was originally called "Six Gun Siding", reminder of its wild west beginnings. The city itself was spread across the center of a plane poetically called the Llano Estacada (the staked plains). Named appropriately by the Spanish conquistadores, it had once been a large inland sea. It was fun to go out to hang my washing and kick over fossils and trilobites etc. Like a large bowl, we were surrounded by 1,000 foot high bluffs.

Tucumcari Mountain

New Mexico Route 66 Tucumcari Tonight
Early Bridge Footings

Tucumcari mountain stood in the center of this bowl, rising to the same height as the surrounding bluffs. According to some of the crusty old timers, the mountain had been named Tucumcari, an Indian name meaning woman's breast, and indeed, if you let your imagination run, that is exactly what it looked like. I remember my husband going on a hiking trip up the mountain one day to discover the wreckage of an old biplane said to have crashed in the '30's during a severe storm.

Although Tucumcari mountain was, by now, just a landmark and a test for the boy scouts for their hiking badges, it had held great religious significance to the local Indians in generations past. They had gathered quite regularly to worship there. The students annually climbed the mountain and re-painted the huge white "T" as a tribute to their agility and honor to the school.

My family's fondest memory of the mountain was one fourth of July when the local Chamber of Commerce had garnered $1,000 and decided to have a spectacular fireworks show from the top of the mountain. We all got in our cars and took our tailgate picnics to gather at the base of the mountain, wait for dark, and enjoy the show. Darkness finally descended to the joy and relief of all the watchers and waiters.

3

The show started with the usual small sky rockets and seemed to be gradually increasing when suddenly, the whole sky was lit with rockets, star bursts, sonic booms and in about five minutes, the show was over! It seems that one of the National Guard helpers couldn't give up his cigar smoking for that period of time. He had leaned over the box of fireworks to choose his next rocket, dropped the cigar and the whole "shooting match" went up in a blaze of glory, short lived to be sure.

—ɯ—

Route 66 from Albuquerque to Tucumcari

The vitality of the city was nurtured by Route 66, (the transcontinental highway), Highway 54 which supplied the local ranchers and shipped stock to Chicago and the Golden State Railroad, a luxurious train trip that went from Chicago to Los Angeles and back. Route 66 has a mystique of its own and in earlier years was the most famous highway in the U.S. The old route still exists and there are always signs along the way and in fact one still exists just a few miles from where I now live and ends at the beginning of the Santa Monica pier. Many cities memorialize the historic old road and I was so pleased to read in Smithsonian magazine the many pages devoted to the story of the resurgence of Route 66 through Arizona. Movies and songs play tribute to it to this day. Television carried various series dealing with Route 66 for a number of years. You could also sing about "getting your kicks on Route 66." On a recent trip to Las Vegas, my daughter and I decided to cut off and take a jaunt on part of the old highway, only to be depressed at seeing all the old buildings closed, crumbled and broken down. We remembered that one of the few entertainment features was "dragging Gaynell (the citie's street name for Route 66)". They spent many evenings just cruising from one end of town to the other, raucous behavior was included. There wasn't much in the way of entertainment for the teenagers.

Tucumcari NM Train Station

The Golden State railway was also very historic and one of our special forms of entertainment was to go down in the afternoon and watch the beautiful train come roaring into the station. That was a big deal for us as entertainment. Most of these locations are now history.

What was it that initially brought the Anglo settlers to Tucumcari?

I often pondered that question. Placed as the city was in the middle of that huge bowl, living at 4300 foot elevation, an exhilarating climate existed; a perfect place to enjoy somewhat allergy free living and healthy high desert weather. It was very arid, desert-like with cactus, tumbleweed and mesquite as the native vegetation. If you ventured up some of the mesas, you found scrubby pine and pinon trees. We would travel there in the fall to gather the pinon nuts.Spreading a blanket underneath the trees, we shooed the kids up into the branches. We vigorously shook the trees and the cones would fall onto the blanket. If the season was just right, a lot of the nuts fell loose and we didn't have to mess with the prickly cones to get at the nuts. They were so sweet and good and I now buy them in large plastic bags at the grocery store, free of the cones. They are labeled "pine nuts" and sell for a good price. One Christmas, I put nuts into small decorated glass jars to send as Christmas gifts to all of our relatives living in "civilized" cities. In an attached note, I related the fact to each one that in the past the Indians extracted the nuts from their formidable shells and made flour out of them as a staple in their diet. It was a basic ingredient in their cooking as they were ground into flour. My sister indicated, after trying to crack the shells for fruit extraction, that she would have starved to death under similar circumstances. On the other hand, my kids would pop them into their mouth, shell and all, and a few cracks later, they had a delicious nut to eat! I, with my fragile teeth, never tried that.

Actually, I am sure the most important drawing factor was the government's implementation in the '30's of the WPA (Work's Progress Administration). This was President Franklin Roosevelt's effort to ease the effects of the depression. Through their efforts, a dam was built across a very deep canyon just about 20 miles from town, where the

Conchas River flowed down from the bluffs. A beautiful lake was formed with a nearly one hundred mile shoreline—Conchas Lake. From that effort they created irrigation for over 40,000 acres, perfect for agriculture as most of the soil was virgin, having never been cultivated. We had corn, cotton, broom corn (the major part of our domestic brooms comes from the product of the broom corn plant) to name a few. Also assorted grains were grown to feed the cattle and horses on the many ranches. One day we were traveling on the highway just outside of town, I commented to the kids that the stuff growing in the field along side of the road was "broom corn". My daughter piped up "Prune corn, prune corn? I thought prunes grew on trees". All of this agriculture created a market for a granary, a cotton gin, cattle fattening pens and a train and highway network to all parts of the country. A fun trip for us and for any of the "visiting firemen" (lots of relatives) was a trip to the cotton gin to watch the huge trucks that had 10-12 feet of wire mesh up the sides from the bed of the truck to hold all the cotton bolls. Our cotton was not like the luxurious Egyptian cotton that has a long staple used to produce very fine material, but it was good enough to create a lively market in cotton sales. The bolls were dumped into the gin which then extracted all the seeds and flotsom and jetsom by literally combing through it to make the cotton marketable.

Naturally, the farmers and ranchers came in abundance. With water readily available in the moisture starved climate, people raised their crops, and provided for their livestock. Many ranches surrounded the area. I remember one Christmas, a parishioner invited us to their ranch to go to their surrounding "forest" of small trees to get our Christmas tree. What an experience. We hiked from the cars along a dry stream bed, up a mesa to where the trees were growing. Each tree became a candidate for chopping down. We finally decided on one particular one and each of the kids had the chance to hack away at it until Jim finally was able to finish cutting it down. We took turns dragging it back to the car. The base of the tree had a diameter almost the size of our little living room but that tree has to have been one of the most memorable we had ever had. To this day, each Christmas as I am shopping for my tree, the wonderful pine scent at the tree lot brings back fond memories of those special days.

So many of the people who settled in Tucumcari were from the deep south, although there was a smattering of people from the "dust bowl" area who had had problems with the years of drought in that part of America. Because of all the agriculture and ranching possibilities, many occupations were required as the city grew. We had the usual lawyers, doctors, teachers, laborers, bankers and Indian Chiefs, no, not really. A perfect cross section of society. We did have some of the Hispanic people in our church. There was a definite division in the Hispanic community between the "misteza" (native Mexicans) and the Castilians who claimed to be descendants from the conquistadores and aristocracy of Spain, the latter being a very proud and productive community. The true native Indians pretty much settled in the western part of the state, Navajos to Gallup and Pueblo Indians to Taos and Santa Fe. Another distinct thriving community just north of the city, up on a mesa was the Mennonites.

They observed all of the clothing customs of their faith, and were incredible farmers and ranchers. There were probably a few hundred of them living in their community and they were so congenial when we encountered them in town. The men work dark pants, white shirts, suspenders and some wore black hats. The women dressed in long cotton dresses with plaited hair and white organdy bonnets. They were always "johnny on the spot" for any emergencies or to help the local farmers and ranchers with their problems. They even conducted training sessions for local people who wanted to farm or had questions about farming skills.

Just a few miles beyond Tucumcari was the ghost town of Tremantina. That was considered a day's trip so we always packed a picnic lunch as there were no stores or restaurants nearby. As a matter of fact, there were no people living there either. We loved walking through the dusty dirt streets, peeking in the deserted windows and trying to recreate in our minds what their lives were like when it was a thriving community. The little one room school house always held a fascination for me. I have no idea what caused the residents to desert or what they had done to keep the community alive in the first place. Water availability, or lack thereof surely had to have something to do with the demise. Apparently the last residents left in 1955.

—ᴍᴍ—

Tucumcari always wanted to be a "Western" town. I mean, <u>really</u> . . . with an original name "Six Gun Siding", imagine the wild history connected to that title! When we moved there, Jim discovered that most of the men wore cowboy boots. He adopted the practice and not only grew him a few inches taller, but cured his foot problems. Due to the fact that the residents represented a wide variety of ethnicities, we could see why they wanted to be Western. Here we were in the middle of a huge prehistoric sea bed, centered by a sacred mountain originally settled by the mestiza. Their names reflected their backgrounds . . . Baca, de Olivera. Along came the Spanish, conquering the Indians and a lot of intermarriage took place. There were those who claimed to be Castilians, still rather haughty and very proud of their Spanish heritage. Macias, Vasquez, Gallegos. Then there were the people from the deep south who were wooed by new opportunity for irrigated farm and ranch land. All in all, this led to a very conservative population. And, as I often reflect, very geographically isolated and therefore quite socially insulated. A perfect example of that mind set was their refusal to accept the Revised Standard version of the Bible which appeared on the scene during our tenure. Our church people, being progressively Presbyterian, had no problems with it as far as we knew, but there was a faction in town that denounced it to the point that they had a big demonstration and burned the RSV bibles on the main street. One old gentleman that confronted Jim about this got very vocal and announced "If the **King James bible** was good enough for Jesus, it's good enough for me!!!"

In order to take advantage of Route 66, the idea was to woo the people off the highway into town to eat, sleep and buy souvenirs. Much of our economy depended on that. When Jim was president of the Chamber of Commerce, he came up with the idea of blocking off the main street and turning it into an "old time" western town. The idea was not received well, but he continued to plug it until he went off the board. It never did materialize.

Downtown Tucumcari—Circa 2006

Sands-Dorsey drug store was the center of town and a gathering place for people wanting to fill their prescriptions, gossip, eat and generally socialize. The soda fountain counter was a real draw. One day, we were there with a group of people when one of the old cowboys drove up in his pickup truck. He was a loud mouthed braggart that everybody really tried to avoid. This particular day, he swaggered in to the drug store and declared that he had a rattlesnake in a milk can in the back of his truck. "Biggest one I ever seen". We all tramped out to the street to see and sure enough, he dumped it onto the bed of the truck, grabbed it behind its head and held it up in the air for us to admire it's eight foot length. I kept way out of reach, you can believe me. Back into the can it went and off he drove. A few weeks later, we heard that he had been a little too casual about picking up a snake. It had turned and bit him on the wrist. He laid close to death in the hospital for a very long time. I don't know how that ever ended up.

The WCTU (Women's Christian Temperance Union) was very active in Tucumcari. For you younger people, this was a group of people who really objected to any form of liquor. During prohibition where it was against the law to drink or possess liquor, they would even go out with hatchets and axes and carve up the illegal barrels of booze. One little elderly lady who was the head of the WCTU in town came to the drug store because she had heard about a new tonic. She had been feeling run down and "Hadacol" had received a lot of publicity. She purchased a quantity and wanted to share the good news with Bob, the owner/pharmacist. She gushed on and on about how much it had helped her and how good she was feeling. We were convulsed with laughter later because the main secret ingredient in that product was alcohol and she was certainly feeling no pain.

The library was our favorite haunt. It was always "climate controlled", which on a hot spring/summer day was an oasis for us to relax after our walk. It was named after Andrew Carnegie, the great national library builder. The two older children, Ricky and Ruth Ann would get home from school about 4 o'clock. We would put Steve in the buggy (there were no such things as strollers in those days) and walk the few blocks to enjoy all the books. Rick had a favorite "Bill and the Clown Bird". It was a delightful story about a boy and his cockatoo. Rick would check it out, take it home to read and return it. Then a few days later he would take it out again! I tried finding a copy a short time ago just to give him for fun! Unfortunately it had long ago gone "out of print". Well, I got on the computer and I did find a collector's copy. Bought and sent it to him for his sixtieth birthday!.

—∞—

Conchas Lake and Dam

Ancient petroglyphs, marine fossils and tales of Spanish Conquistadors mark the past of Conchas Lake. Historical significance is the construction of Conchas Dam from 1935-1939 by the WPA (Works Progress Administration) during Franklin Roosevelt's New Deal era. Conchas Dam became the 17th dam project built by the U.S. Army Corps of Engineers and the first district in New Mexico was established here.

New Mexico is appropriately called "The Land of Enchantment" and it did have that power. Going to Conchas Lake made us so aware of the stark beauty of this land. The canyon carved out by the ancient river, dammed to contain the water was, to me, a real enchantment. There was some vegetation, primarily small, scrubby pine trees that we appreciated for some shade. Going there was pure pleasure and relaxation. Jim and I would load up the kids, the swimgear, lots of beverages and food and head out the twenty miles to spend the day. We had a special spot that was at the edge of the lake, a cliff about ten feet above the water. We could jump or dive in with our inner tubes, hook our feet on the tube in front of you and make a five tube train to paddle up and down the lake. What a way to spend the day! In between paddling sessions, we would eat our picnic lunch, nap, enjoy the scenery or practice our diving. Needless to say, we were usually pretty sunburned by the time we dragged ourselves home in the early evening, totally relaxed and reenergized.

An interesting site that we discovered on one of our paddling trips was an area that had been a deserted Penetente cemetery. We could see a few gravestones, in bad shape, but still there. They had been saved when the dam was built as it was just slightly above the water line. We knew it was Penetente because of the three crosses marking the site. Los Penetentes roots in America date back more than 1000 years to the Flagellantes (beating oneself in submission) orders of the Catholic Church in Spain and Italy. The Penetente church in America was originally formed in 1794 in Tumacacori, Arizona, by a Franciscan priest who had come from Spain. The practices of that branch of the faith had been adopted and distorted over many years by the native population at the top of what was called "The Plaza", a winding road up the mountain just outside Santa Fe. You travel through communities named Chama, Truchas, and Chimayo . . . wonderful poetic names, until you reach the pinnacle at Penasco. The isolation caused by the geography of the area had created this atmosphere of isolation and the Catholic people there gradually adopted the Penetente form of catholicism. Each year on Maunday Thursday, the men of the church would gather in the sanctuary where they had placed a large wooden cross on the floor. They stood on it in the dark, swaying back and forth, rocking the cross and passing a rock from hand to hand. When the cross stopped swaying, whoever was holding the rock, was the "chosen one" to be crucified on the next day, Good Friday. It was considered an honor. How we became aware of all of this is that the Presbyterian Church had a small hospital in Cleveland, a few miles away and every Good Friday, these worshipers would bring the "Honoree" down to the hospital to be cared for.

He had the nail holes in his hands and feet and would be suffering from what was the usual cause of death on the cross . . . the lungs collapse from the body weight. Well, before we arrived in Tucumcari, they had long since been censured by the higher-ups of the Roman Catholic Church and told they would be excommunicated if they continued to practice the life taking process. They then managed to take the man down before he died and bring him in—nail holes in hands and feet, but able to be saved. Google "Encounter with the Penetentes". It records Charles Lummis' (famous writer) experience of surreptitiously filming one of the crucifixions.

Another fascinating church in the plaza area was "El Sanctuario". It was a typical adobe building with adjacent buildings attached. When we walked in, we were stunned by the thousands of crutches, braces, and every kind of medical device hanging from the ceilings and walls. Images of La Virgen de Gualupe gathered supplicants as she is considered a patron of the Americas. The locals call the church "The church of the holy mud". The Archdiocese of Santa Fe calls it "the Lourdes of America". Averaging some 200,000 visitors visiting each year made it a real point of interest for us. Called "el pocito" by the locals, it reflected the story that 200 years ago a friar saw a strange light near the Santa Cruz river. He began to dig to locate the source and uncovered a crucifix. He took it to a nearby church, but each time it was taken there, it mysteriously returned to the place where it had been found. A chapel was built in 1913 at that spot. The dirt is considered sacred with healing powers. In the center of what apparently had been the sanctuary was a large hole with people sitting on the edges. They would scoop out the sand and rub it on whatever area they were seeking healing for. Many were putting the sand into containers to take with them. The sand in the hole is replaced every day. When we were there, the buildings were filled with people. There were chanting sounds hanging in the air and I got a real sense of the deep faith of these people in their miracles. I have an etching on my living room wall that reminds me of that church.

I was fortunate to be able to participate in monthly meetings of the women in the Presbytery. We met in various church locations around the state. My most memorable one was in Chama where on a freezing cold day, we had our meeting in a small room in order to stay warm in January. The women were on a money raising drive to get heating for the sanctuary! I was so humbled by this and the fact that I had only to turn a switch in my house and in the church to be warm as toast. The Plaza area became one of my favorite meeting places.

Ghost Ranch was one of our most exciting vacation spots. The history of the whole place was intriguing. In 1955, Arthur and Phoebe Pack donated to the Presbyterian Church over 20,000 acres of wild plains and mountains that had been their dude ranch and home since 1936. The original land grant had come from the King of Spain in 1766 and was called Piedra Lumbre or "shining rock". Tales of ghosts and legends of hangings existed and the camp leaders often told the stories to the wide eyed kids there on vacation. As we left Santa Fe, headed north to Abiquiu for the few miles to the ranch, we were always awe struck by the incredible natural beauty. The highest hill was crowned with what was named "Chimney Rock" and that became the goal of a lot of the hiking groups. Classes covering everything from theology, crafts and hiking adventures were offered. We ate in a huge dining room served cafeteria style with lots of good food and fun friends. When the kids were old enough, they stayed in the teepees up on the mesa, but Jim and I always opted for a cabin with NICE BEDS. A massive landslide had occurred in the ancient history of the area, creating an immense bowl where the forest ranger and various locals would present programs and shows for the tourists. A visit to the Pack Museum on the highway was a MUST. At one point, they had built an extension to the building to house a family of beavers. A stream was diverted to run through the building and the beavers had built a dam. We could watch them in action due to a glass wall that went from ceiling to floor and didn't disturb their activity.

Our path for one of the hikes to Chimney Rock took us past Georgia O'Keeffe's home that had been give to her in the late 40's by Mr. Pack. She named it Rancho los Burros. It was right in the center of the ranch and easy to find, but she was extremely reclusive and had been guaranteed privacy. So much of her art work reflects the scenery from around her house. In fact, a friend and neighbor had given her the skull of his pet steer that had died. She included it in one of her paintings and that became the permanent logo for Ghost Ranch. Jim wore a silver ring with the steer logo for many years and my daughter now has it. As we walked past Ms. O'keefe's high wall one day, we could see her companion in the back yard, but only his face and black hat. It was hard not to peek to see if we would discover her at any time.

When Jim was a counselor, he had taken a group of teenagers on a hike over one of the mesas. The hike was going well until they came to a hill. They started to climb with Jim in the lead. As he crowned the hill he saw a rather large bear on the other side. He came thundering back down to where the group was starting their ascent, waving his arms and yelling "Bear, Bear". They got the message and all made a quick retreat back to the more civilized part of the ranch. Wild animal encounters were common.

A number of years ago, Jim and I traveled to Ghost Ranch for him to attend a conference. I spent some time at the old Abiquiu Inn because of its history and exquisite enchiladas. I managed to go there every noon time to have lunch while Jim was busy. I noticed a large adobe-type building up on the mesa behind the Inn and decided to explore. It had been purchased by an Islamic group and they had created an ashram. One of the members (a young, blonde headed convert) took me on a tour of the buildings and I was really impressed, having no knowledge about muslims. Now, with the religious/military climate what it is, I find myself to be quite upset as I found out that they had bought the City of Abiquiu. Apparently, now, it is only used for retreats.

True to the ranching history of the area, crops were planted and ranchers took care of them and the livestock that they had on the ranch. I was allergic to alfalfa and had to avoid the big central office building as the field across form the entrance was planted totally to alfalfa.

To give some idea of the climate there, we were in shirt sleeves each day in the hot dry weather, but by sundown, it got pretty cool. In fact, one evening, one of the counselors had parked his VW bug in front of the office. When he went next morning to drive it, the motor just growled and growled and wouldn't start. When he opened the hood, he discovered a huge rattlesnake completely coiled around the engine having been wooed by the warm interior.

There was an air of tranquility about Tucumcari. It might have been due to living at higher altitude or possibly the fact that we were so geographically isolated from any other forms of civilization. As we were half way between two metropolitan-type cities, the people had formed their own rules and regulations. Our dear friend Jerry was a highway patrolman and was well aware of the exhilaration people experienced as they came through our area. On top of that, these tourists had driven a number of miles to get there and were tired. Jerry was a feisty Irishman who became a very good friend of Jim's. When he was on duty and a car would come barreling down from the mesa, roaring through town on Gaynell Avenue (Route 66), he would pull them over and give them three levels of lecture. #1—at ten miles over the speed limit, "Slow down and save lives". #2—at twenty miles over the speed limit, he gave them a hefty ticket. #3—Anything beyond that, he stopped them, opened the driver's door, snatched the driver out and yelled "Now you've jeopardized MY life". Off to jail.

If there was a lot of crime in Tucumcari, I wasn't aware of it. The newspaper would report an occasional traffic accident, a lost pet, etc. but I don't remember reading about or experiencing any crime that I am sure existed at some level. Our news came to us through our local paper, our radio or the intrusive television. I remember that we pretty much only watched the game shows or children oriented sitcoms until the children went to bed. Jim was away most evenings for church meetings, so I particularly liked the game shows and I Love Lucy. One day, I became fascinated with the news of a man named Fidel Castro and his sidekick Che Guevara who had slogged through the mountains and jungles of Cuba to free their island country. It took awhile and was the talk of the town. I watched faithfully each day to the point of neglecting my household duties. I cheered with great gusto when he finally "freed" his people. We looked at him as a great saviour to a downtrodden people. The excessive, opulent living of the ruling parties was exposed and we were all flabbergasted. Then finally when Castro was exposed for who he really represented, we went through the Cuban missile crisis and felt not only fear, but great pride in President Kennedy's handling of the wholesituation. So much for the usual tranquility.

The crimes of the community were often between family members. One altercation took place at a fence line between two brothers' ranches. Each man was demanding what he considered HIS property. The discussion became a heated argument and the one rancher pulled out a gun and shot his brother dead! What a way to settle an argument. THAT hit the news!!

A tragedy occurred when two twelve year old boys took up a rifle and went off to play. They didn't realize the gun was loaded and the one boy accidentally shot his friend who died. There was some heated discussion about all of this in the community and the surviving boy suffered from severe guilt to the point where he hung himself and also died. We didn't even know the boys, but fully suffered the families grief. Real sad!

—⚋—

Holiday Blizzard—Route 66

Sunset Time—Tucumcari Mountain

The weather in Tucumcari was probably the most IDEAL I have experienced. There were four distinct seasons. Coming from California, though having been raised in Wisconsin, I was enchanted by the fact that each season lasted just three months with an occasional "rogue" snowstorm in April that managed to kill the fruit that had just started to set. Summers were unbearably hot with each day becoming a blistering, dry 114 or so degrees on occasion. Life was only bearable indoors with a "swamp cooler" in the window. We had to wear gloves to touch the wheel of a car and were parboiled before the air conditioner (if you were lucky enough to have one) tuned up. At 5:00 or so, a breeze would come up to cool us off and we almost always slept under something, at least a sheet. Each year about Thanksgiving, we awoke to find that we had our first snow storm. Actually the snow was more like popcorn, dry and huge flakes. At the first sign of a flake or two, you turned on the radio to listen to all the announcements of events that were being cancelled. Immediately after the snow storm had hit in our first winter, I asked when the snow plows would come out to clear the streets (logical question from a midwesterner) and was told that the city owned no snow plows. Why bother to plow when you knew it would melt in a few days!! So the whole town, except for the milk trucks, took a vacation! No one went anywhere. Our houses were isolated cocoons of warmth within a white world. The milk truck came up and down the streets selling food supplies for those who were foolish enough not to have their freezers well stocked!! Neighbors all gathered and put sleds behind the four wheel vehicles so the parents and kids alike could ride the sleds up and down the empty streets. The first day or so the snow was too dry for snowball fights, but as it warmed up it got sticky and I remember my husband building a marvelous igloo for the kids. Actually, I think he and I enjoyed it more than they did!

My feet were freezing as I trudged down the hall on a particularly frigid, blustery morning at 2 A.M. My son Steve had awakened with, what I assumed was a nightmare. I finally got him settled back down to sleep, headed back down the hall to our bedroom. An aside here. When I get up in the night, I have to take a trip to the bathroom, so as I staggered along, I gradually lowered my pajama bottoms, rounded the corner into the bathroom and plunked down on the facility. My husband was sitting there!!

Finally, with the coming of spring, all the trees budded out and the rain storms arrived. When I saw the distinctive clouds begin to gather, I would call the kids and we lined up, sitting on our "lean to" porch with our backs up against the front wall of the house to watch the storm gather. What a display! The lightning shows were remarkable. When the rain finally came and we were getting wet, the weaker of us went inside, but mostly we would play in the rain, depending on the temperature. When the rain stopped and the usual rainbow formed, sometimes double, we hopped in the car and headed for the countryside to see the arroyos flooded. There was a genus of tree toad that hibernated deep in the soil and only came to "life" when it rained, so the desert floor was alive with little hoppy toads, the size of your thumbnail. Imagine the fun the kids had gathering these prizes to take home and keep for awhile.

One evening, as we had lost interest in the storm and were more interested in eating our dinner, lightning struck the meter box just a few feet from where we were enjoying our ham salad sandwiches and soup. It took quite a while to find Ruth Ann's sandwich, which she threw into the air as she screamed and headed for the base of the dining room table. The sandwich had landed on top of the refrigerator.

Storms like I had never seen before were commonplace. One summer day, we were invited to go on a picnic with our "forest" friends. We weren't able to go, but they did. Since it appeared to be a nice day, they proceeded to take their pickup truck down to drive the dry arroyo with the back packed with food, drinks and kids. Suddenly, there was a flash flood with torrents of water coursing down the arroyo bed. The wall of water and debris smashed into the pickup, lifting it and carrying it down stream about two miles before it finally lodged in the side of the canyon. Everyone was okay, somewhat bruised and battered but all the food was gone and the truck destroyed. A lesson learned.

Jim had a similar experience after he had delivered me to be a counselor at a church camp in Taos. He brought our youngest child, Steve, with him for the trip. On the way home they came to an arroyo that was running with a small amount of water. Jim went ahead and entered the dip in the road when a wall of water surged down and hit the car. The car didn't move, but it rapidly filled with water as high as the seats. His camera, wallet etc., and he and Steve were all soaked. The flow of water slowed down and he opened the car doors to let the flood of water out. They finally limped back to Tucumcari to dry out.

Fall was a glorious blaze of color and the balmy weather with the aspens in the local mountains turning yellow, the sage, purple and the sunsets like nothing I had ever seen before or since. The first year I tried recording all this with a camera, but soon gave up as I ran out of room to keep the beautiful pictures. We raked the leaves, leaped in and out until we were exhausted. Steve loved to leap into the piles of leaves with our dog screaming "Banzai". How I miss the leaf burning time. No smog to worry about then and the smell was unforgettable. To this day, I wait anxiously to recapture that special change in the air and sky that precedes the coming of autumn.

Mrs. S was a teacher and a close neighbor with many mulberry trees in her yard. They were always like a magnet to the children. She was comfortable with kids so she let them climb up her trees and eat until they were sick! So many of their clothes were permanently polka dotted with mulberry stains from Mrs. S's trees. The local farmers sold their produce and our little garden would start to fade away, although the zucchini seemed to go on forever. I canned as much of this bounty as I had energy and room for. What a joy to take part in the consumption of the "fruits of my labors" throughout the year.

It was a well known fact that the weather man was a direct employee of the Chamber of Commerce. Route 66 was the choice of routes to take to the Rose Bowl each year as it appeared to be far enough south to avoid bad weather. It was the quickest way from Michigan, Illinois or whoever it was that was playing as the Big Ten team that year. Usually, the pilgrims would come through about Christmas time in order to be there in L.A. in plenty of time for New Years Day. We always managed to have one of our worst snow storms just in time to catch the weary travelers. All the motels filled up and the restaurants were swamped. The merchants sold half their merchandise during that time! Needless to say, we loved the commercial opportunities for our little community. Well, one year, it was so bad and the crowd stranded was so huge that a plea went out on the radio for locals to be willing to take people into their homes as the Army Reserve building and schools were full of people who had to sleep on the floor. We immediately packed up the family and headed for the Armory to pick up "our family". As soon as we got in the building and noticed this one family, we knew that we were probably the only ones who would choose them. The husband was an army Sergeant, and the wife was Japanese with two lovely little boys. We took them home and settled them in. She was a native of Hiroshima and, in fact, had lost her family in their atomic holocaust. She spoke almost no English but offered to cook our dinner. We went off to the market and with gesturing and picture drawing, we got supplies for an oriental dinner which she cooked and which we thoroughly enjoyed. Believe me, there were no Asian restaurants in town. While she and I were working in the kitchen, I became aware of the kids watching a movie on TV and came around the corner of the living room to find that it was an old war movie. My son was on his knees, screaming "Kill them Japs, kill them dirty Japs". Where's a gag when you need one! Despite this unfortunate occurrence, they stayed for three days and we enjoyed their company.

When we first moved to town, we were "put up" in what had been a tarpaper shack formerly used for storage by the church. It was called "The Manse". Ah, yes, the manse—dictionary description is "the house and land occupied by a minister or parson—root word MANSION). Parts had been added periodically and it became a HOUSE. Admittedly, there were three bedrooms, but unfortunately, in order to get to the bathroom, we had to go through Ruth Ann's lean-to bedroom. Her roof slanted to the point that she had to use caution when sitting up in bed. The heater provided was a massive furnace under the floor between the living and dining room. When it belched forth its contents, the metal grate was so hot, many of us sustained blisters if walking over it. Of course, covering the grate with a rug defeated the original purpose of dispensing heat. In summer, you can bet I kept a rug over it to prevent varmints from coming to visit. The immediate area around the large grate was overly warm while the outer edges of the house remained frigid all winter. We spent a lot of wintertime huddled in the living/dining room. When we first arrived with all our belongings not too far behind, inside the house we found various scattered pieces of furniture here and there that been donated. Our guides to the home were not very pleased with the fact that we had been married for many years and had a house full of furniture as a result. They rather grudgingly removed the items but I did manage to keep the old round oak dining table and mirrored sideboard (which incidentally, I hated leaving behind when we left as it was a true relic, eligible for Antiques Roadshow). When various people came to help us settle in, a few helpers were astonished and very vocal about all the sturdy packing boxes I had garnered from the local liquor store before packing up. I assured them, emptying all those bottles had been very difficult for us!!! The house was placed in the center of the church property, surrounded by the office, education building and sanctuary. When the new manse was built, the community all gathered to watch the old house put up on round logs and towed down the main drag to be placed a few miles out of town on Route 66. It became the office for a sleazy motel with a questionable reputation. (By the way, on a return trip in 2006, the house was still there serving the same purpose it had in 1963). Our backyard was often used for church functions. One day, my dear husband came into the kitchen where I was cooking dinner. He walked up behind me, slid his arms around me and proceeded to kiss me on the neck. I stiffened like I was frozen—for standing outside the window looking in was the entire girl scout troop!

On a lovely summer weekend, our high school group decided they wanted to raise some money. Their idea was to have a backyard BBQ. They managed to buy a pig, vegies et al which they then placed in a pit they had dug. They built a big fire and waited until coals were formed, put the pig and all the food into the pit, and lo and behold, by six that evening, we were serving BBQ to all the invited guests. They made a lot of money and gained a lot of admiration from the community.

One of our most loyal families were ranchers. Mr. B at one point decided that the existing manse was not befitting the status of our church in this town and went forward to see about building a new house. He finally found a vacant piece of property in the newer and more genteel area of town, wangled the owner into selling it to the church and proceeded to hit up everyone in town for some commitment to this new venture of his. Sure enough, he was able to raise enough money to build a lovely, three bedroom house, which we were the first to occupy. (Incidentally, it still stands and is occupied by the current pastor). When we moved from the old house, we borrowed a pick-up truck. Steve, then two years old, sat in the front seat. I jumped out of the truck after parking it close to the front door to get something out of the back. Steve somehow or other, managed to release the gear shift and the truck rolled into the corner of the front door, leaving a dent which we hastily had repaired!

One of the things that was not taken care of was "thought about the yard". Neither Jim nor I have a green thumb, so it remained an area scattered only with scrubby orphan trees, ankle high weeds and lots of dirt. I casually mentioned it to Mr. B and he immediately responded that what that lawn needed was fertilizer. Jim had gone that week to be a counselor at one of our church camps and would be gone for about ten days. I figured we would wait until he returned to face the problem. Unfortunately, Mr. B had other plans. At four o'clock the following bleary morning, the phone rang and I was greeted with Mr. B's boisterous voice saying "Aren't you up yet?" I groaned and said "What can I do to help you?" He informed me that his workers were on their way with the fertilizer he had promised!! "Would you please meet them outside in the front yard". I threw on a robe and dashed out the front door, in the dark, to find a huge dump truck, backing up to the curb and gradually raising the truck bed to deposit a full load of steaming manure (freshly obtained, I am sure). It lay in a mountain shaped pile with fumes exuding from all sides. The driver said we just needed to spread it out over the lawn and we would enjoy beautiful grass. I went back into the house, crashed into bed, and prayed for Jim's quick return. Well, that didn't happen and the massive mountain remained where it had been dumped. Summer was in full bloom and the full day's sun shone down on the pile. It got to the point where I had to keep the windows closed 24/7 to survive. My neighbors started bugging me about it, but I didn't know what to do. The die was cast when my next door neighbor called to exclaim "THERE'S SOMETHING DEAD IN THERE!!" Well, I would have been a fool not to acknowledge that fact and so I started with a shovel and mask to spread as much as I could handle. Jim got home in a few days and it took us at least one week to spread the reeking mass over the yard.

THE GRASS NEVER GREW IN THAT SPOT AGAIN.

First Presbyterian Church

The church was a magnificent structure, on a corner lot just a few blocks from the downtown. It had been built with large blocks of red sandstone, cut from the local hills. Built by the pioneer Presbyterians in the late 1800's, it started life as a mission church. The sanctuary was built "in the round" with individual chairs of wrought iron slats and velvet seat backs and cushions. There were even arm rests. The ceiling was made of white embossed tin squares that had flying cupids adorning the edges. The choir loft held as many as ten singers and the organ was adjacent to the loft. A newer building which housed the office and Sunday School rooms with an auditorium had been added to make the buildings form a "U" with the manse in the center front. Legend had it that the church had once proudly sported a tall, pointed tower and spire, but apparently that had disappeared in a severe storm sometime in the distant past. The stained glass windows were definitely of the old school with pictures of Jesus with the children etc. The colors were very vibrant in spite of their age.

The organ probably was very old and in fact, one evening, Jim received a phone call from the choir director with the alarming news that smoke was coming from the organ. Because Jim knew that it was probably on its last legs and hoping the insurance would cover replied "Let it burn". It didn't and it actually was still functioning when we left.

By the time we left Tucumcari, the church had been condemned by the city and the workers came to tear it all down. Since we couldn't bear to watch the destruction, we left the day before. To begin the destructive process, the workers went up above the ceiling and clipped ONE guy wire. Whereupon, the entire ceiling collapsed to the floor below. Good thing it hadn't happened when Mr. J had gone to church. Mr. J was the local banker and always sat in the very same seat each Sunday with his wife and young son. He was very stoical and formal in his demeanor and usually nodded off during the sermon. One particular Sunday, a piece of the ceiling decided to fall and land on Mr. J's head. The following Sunday, he was seated in a different seat!

Mr. B decided that he wanted to help out our small choir as we were very short of singers. He contributed a good voice and was a strong supporter of our group efforts. One Icelandic Sunday morning, as we sat in the front row of the choir loft, preparing to enjoy the sermon, we were suddenly aware of a strong, cold breeze. Jim's robe was flapping at the lectern and we all started looking around to figure out what window was broken or door left open. It finally dawned on all of us in the loft, that Mr. B had crossed his legs during the sermon, slumped down to doze and in the process had bumped the air conditioner switch and we were enjoying an unseasonable summer cool down.

"The Transients of Tucumcari"—sounds like a Broadway musical, doesn't it. Unfortunately, it was one of the most obvious social problems of the city. Situated halfway between Amarillo and Albuquerque, with very little hospitable territory in between, people traveling from coast to coast managed to get on Route 66 on their way to or from Chicago. We were inundated with individuals and families—all looking for a handout. The city finally got the brilliant idea of turning this problem over to the many churches in town and a group of all the clergy in town formed the Ministerial Alliance, which depended on donated funds from residents of the city. Jim happened to be the president of said organization and was in charge of the distribution of money. We came up with the idea of "chits", pieces of paper which sent the transient to a preselected grocery store, drug store or gas station for whatever it was that they needed or asked for. Because Jim was out of the office a good deal of the time and there was no full time secretary, he had the bright idea of giving the "chits" to me to distribute. We lived in the north part of town, so people would drive to our house and I would give them the appropriate "chit". One day, I heard the doorbell ring. As I approached the screen door, I could see that the person awaiting me was a very dirty, disreputable, evidently intoxicated man who asked me for gas to get to California. I looked past him to the dilapidated car in my driveway and noticed three other dirty, disreputable men in the car. I got a little anxious and decided to get rid of them as fast as possible, as I was alone in the house. I wrote out the gas "chit" for $10.00 and he thanked me and they drove away. As was my usual habit, I called the gas station to forewarn them that "an old car with four men" was on its way for gas. A few minutes later, my phone rang. When I answered it, the man on the other end was laughing hysterically. It was Rod, the gas station attendant. He, between gasps for breath, informed me that the car actually contained three men and a DOG!!

Some of the "funnest" conversations Jim and I would have at the end of the day would be about the daily parade of transients coming through town. One group of two women and numerous children were from a circus. The two women were "the tattooed ladies". In those days, tattoos were very rare, but they were delighted to remove items of clothing to show Jim their "claim to fame". The children were really rag-tag and dirty, in various sizes and shapes, including a baby in the one woman's arms (the real sympathy "getter"). They drove up to the church in a beat up old car and the kids poured out like the Toonerville Trolley. Jim later got calls from a number of the churches saying this same group had been to their locations also. When they left with their "chits", Jim got curious and followed them to find them getting into their OTHER car a few blocks away. He watched them drive off in the old clunker and a very slick, new Cadillac!

Jim really backed off after that incident. A man came to the church and said he would be willing to work for food (does that sound familiar? At least his effort wasn't for beer !) Jim put him to work at the front of the office pulling weeds and turning over the soil. Within no time at all, the man was at the door declaring that he had hurt his back and couldn't continue. A few weeks later, Jim was confronted by a lawyer, claiming his client was suing for physical damages!! We had lawyers in our church and fortunately for us, the suit never went to court.

—∭—

I am reminded of the process of growing things in Tucumcari. When we moved to the new house, the soil had never been cultivated and, though there was a layer of "caliche" (clay) soil, it was virgin and things grew well. Below the kitchen window, I had planted dahlias, a new plant in my vocabulary. They grew to be almost as tall as some shrubs and the flowers were as big as salad plates. They framed the kitchen window so that I could see them when doing dishes, a task I disliked. We planted an apricot tree just outside that same window and if we were lucky enough to not have our annual blizzard at Easter time, we had wonderful fruit, my favorite to enjoy. I, being of the exotic mind, planted three kinds of tomatoes—big, round red ones, tiny red ones and yellow ones that were shaped like pears. They made good snacks for the kids and delightfully graced my salads.

One year the kids were enjoying a watermelon, sitting on the curb in front of the house. I had planted marigolds that took over the whole corner of the lot and grew to immense size. Naturally, they spit the seeds into the marigold bed and lo and behold, a watermelon plant volunteered. When we finally discovered it, one melon was pretty good sized and we carefully covered it with marigold branches so no one could find it. It finally got ripe and we had a backyard picnic to celebrate, eating it for dessert.

I was greeted at the door by a farmer friend and thought he had brought me vegetables. He smiled a big smile and handed me a bag, commenting that this was something we could have for dinner. After I had thanked him and he left, I opened the bag to find four dead ducks, still with feathers. I was grateful for his generosity, but I had to give them to a friend who knew how to deal with them! He prepared them and we all enjoyed our duck dinner together. Many of the local truck farmers had developed good businesses selling fresh vegetables door to door. A man I didn't recognize came to my door to show me the wonderful variety of home grown goodies he had to offer. He was Hispanic and I was a bit uncomfortable because he was staring so boldly at me. Finally in halting English he said "What color are your eyes? I've never seen green eyes before!" He became my regular supplier of fresh vegies.

—⟋⟋⟍—

Though we chase an occasional racoon or possum from our garbage dumpster and periodically run across a coyote, skunk or bear here in the San Gabriel foothills, it cannot in anyway be compared to the wildlife in Tucumcari. When we arrived in town, about the only wild thing my kids had ever seen outside of the zoo were squirrels

The elk were abundant and there was a hunting season for them each fall. Hunting was a real boon to the local people, as they really did process and eat the meat they had killed. The law said that no shots could be fired within a distance of five miles either side of the road during hunting season. Needless to say, those animals were smart. They must have gotten the memo because they would gather in large herds well within the five mile limit until hunting season was over, allowing us to view the animals grazing peacefully with no fear of the hungry hunters.

Jim was returning one night from a conference and was coming down off the mesa near Trementina. A car came racing past him and Jim was concerned because he knew that the cattle came onto the road at night. The road is open range which meant there were no fences to contain the livestock. The asphalt is still warm from the day's sunshine and a magnet for the animals to bed down. Sure enough, within minutes,

Jim saw the brakes lights come on and the car slammed to a stop. The driver waited until Jim came along to lead him slowly around all the cows until they got back into town. One unlucky driver we talked to had slammed into a cow and it had completely destroyed his car.

Mr. B ranched here outside of Tucumcari, in Santa Rosa, New Mexico, and also in Texas. His herds were sheep and cattle, some Santa Gertrudis cattle (an extremely sturdy cross breed of brahman and beef shorthorn cattle developed in the King Ranch in Texas). He always had the most exotic pets. One year his kids had a boa constrictor, long before snakes were considered popular pets. The poor thing made the mistake of crawling between the screen and the winter storm window. They missed him, but couldn't find him 'til springtime—he had frozen to death in the winter. Their dearest pet was a wild javelina (type of wild boar) that they discovered on a trip across the hills. She was immediately named "Harriet, the Havelina" and grew from about one pound to 25-30 formidable pounds on the good food given her by the family. She was most affectionate, noisy and playful. Her coat was anything but comforting if you can imagine a Fuller brush—those are boar bristles, or at least, were in that day and age. When she got to a fairly good size and was knocking over the tables and people, she was sent to the San Antonio zoo where she may still be.

One of our unusual pets were my son Rick's tarantulas. He was fascinated by their docile nature and knew that they were different from the poisonous South American banana tarantulas. He was often seen with one of them perched on his shoulder and believe me, everyone kept clear of him at that time! Every fall, the tarantulas would migrate. They were about the size of a saucer in diameter and as they crossed the highways at their snails-pace, the cars would demolish them in no time flat (figuratively speaking!). One day, Ruth Ann invited her friend Clara over to play and wanted to show off Rick's collection of tarantulas. They went to the box Rick kept them in, opened the lid to show the full box and since I was standing there, I looked in, too. Image my shock to find her thumb clutching the lid just about two inches away from a walnut sized black widow spider! Some pet!

When we had been settled for just a short time, the front door flew open and Rick was shoving a prehistoric monster in front of my eyes. My first impression was "If I pass out, he may reconsider his bold actions", but good old Mary kept her cool and calmly stated "What a lovely looking lizard". Rick immediately went into a biological diatribe letting me know that this was a horned toad and that when it got mad, it could "spit blood". He then turned this two inch long monster over on its back, stroked it's soft tummy and literally hypnotized it. I often found myself over the years, picking them up lovingly, holding them upright and then turning them over to do the same thing!

The day Rick came home from school with a ghastly, skeletal stray dog on a rope, I knew the old story "She followed me home, can we keep her?" Route 66 (Gaynell Avenue) was the local dumping spot for unwanted pets. No SPCA there! People would just turn them out as they passed through, and if they could survive, many found homes in the community. This poor pup had lived on a very sturdy type of gourd that grew wild in the ditches alongside the roads. We took her in and because of her red coat and "questionable" background, we gave her a good biblical name, "Jezebel". That little pup grew to pony size!! I should have looked at her paws and would have guessed. Anyway, the manse, situated as it was, was so close to the church and education building with our back yard also the church's front yard. On a particular Sunday morning, I noticed a gathering of elders looking into the yard, counting the dog piles, which I am sure they took no time to report to the congregation. Jezzy's favorite spot for loitering was on Rick's bed, stretched out full length with her head placed comfortably on his pillow.

It was a lovely spring Saturday, so I had invited the elders and families to a picnic in our back yard (which had been scrupulously cleaned by then) and we had a lovely barbecue. That morning, I had made three of my special, scrumptious "soda cracker pies" with fresh picked peaches and real whipped cream. They were on the kitchen table, waiting until we had eaten to dig in. I was floored to walk into the kitchen to get the pies and make a grand entrance only to discover Jezebel, up on her hind legs, gleefully licking all the whipped cream off one of the pies. I had to really cut small slices in the remaining untouched pies in order for each of us to have "just a taste".

When we moved, we gave Jezebel to a local sheep rancher and later found out that, because she chased the sheep, he had shot her and hung her hide on his fence. Really civilized!

The older kids in the neighborhood often went hunting out on the sage covered prairie, mostly for rabbits. One day, here came Rick with his shirt full of wriggling baby jackrabbits. Their ears were far longer than their whole body and it was a wonder that their size didn't cause them to topple over by sheer weight. He and his buddies had killed a rabbit, not knowing it was a "mama" but they soon found the hole with the three little bunnies. Rick was devastated so he built a lovely cage for them and they seemed very happy. In the meantime, he had been thoroughly scratched on his chest bringing them home and I, suspecting some kind of lethal rabbit fever, brought out the merthiolate to paint the scratch marks. Well, also having a slight artistic bent, I made a lovely merthiolate outline of a rabbit with big ears. A few hours later, Rick came moaning in to me to show me that he was allergic to the merthiolate and had puffed up at least half an inch on each lovely stroke I had made. He went swimming at the community pool in a tee shirt for many weeks!

Our most exotic pet was a baby skunk. Given to us by a local farmer, the mother was the victim of a traffic accident. We called her "Fiorella", translated "Little flower" ala Walt Disney. She was so tiny, only a pound or so. She had been de-scented and had a big fluffy tail. She wandered all over the house and would climb into our laps when we sat down. She would go around and around in a circle and wrap her voluminous tail around herself to sleep. She was so dear, but we never were able to completely get rid of the smell and it <u>was</u> offensive. As per usual, we gave her to a local farmer who loved having her and apparently had no sense of smell!!

On summer evenings, all the neighbor kids gathered under the corner street light to watch and catch exotic bugs. We grown ups would flake out on our front porch and watch. We were well entertained by the antics. Rick one night caught an emerald beetle, a little over one inch in length. He tied a string to one of its legs and it would fly around like a model airplane. Those bugs were startlingly beautiful, with a heavy scarab-like shell of a bright metallic green. What a treat to see.

—✺—

I have always been a lover of food. We used to joke and say that I was born "tired and hungry". Well, New Mexico was an eye opener for me in that department. With a Norwegian father and German mother, the food I had enjoyed growing up was really bland. This food was so entirely different than any we had known and to this day, I try to locate a restaurant that can equal the unique flavors of New Mexican food. Some people say it comes from the Sonoran area of Mexico. I buy only New Mexican chili powders as I have never found any to equal. I finally have found a restaurant in Sierra Madre that makes enchiladas very similar to those I loved in Tucumcari.

My first exposure to the local food was a sunny day when Ricky and Ruth Ann were in school and Steven Paul was not yet two years old. I popped him into our buggy and took off for a walk up to Gaynell Avenue (Route 66). It was the commercial center of the county and solid on each side of the highway with restaurants, motels and curio shops. I headed for the restaurant that was owned by an older couple in our church. They also had a motel. When I reached the restaurant and was seated, I started examining the menu. I KNEW then, that I was in a foreign country. The one item that intrigued me the most was the "guacamole", which I of course mispronounced. The waiter described it. I may have eaten an avocado in something, at sometime in my life but certainly was not aware of it. Being from the meat and cheese eating state of Wisconsin contributed to my lack of awareness. The guacamole came with incredible chips, also new to me. Needless to say, I was hooked at first swallow and have been enamored ever since.

The next venture into this new gastronomic world was a trip to "La Cita" (which incidentally is still there, but was closed for repairs on our last trip). There I discovered the ethereal beauty of eating a sopapilla!! It sort of resembles a raised doughnut, but a slightly heavier texture, puffed up like a pillow (for which it gets it's name), hollow and warm. Tear off a corner and drizzle in the honey and you know you have been transported to gastronomic heaven! Of course you end up with honey dripping down your chin but are delighted to lick it off. NO ONE in the outer civilized world of California makes sopapillas (other than a very poor imitation in which they fry up a tortilla—yuck!). Needless to say, I got the recipe from someone and made them on many occasions. Our last trip was spent eating sopapillas at EVERY MEAL. The problem with filling up on their delicious food was that the owner at La Cita, Maurice, made the most delicious PIES. I finally learned to hold back on the food I could take home in a doggie bag so that I could manage to cram in a piece of warm pie that had been made from whatever local fruit was fresh.

The Martinez family owned one of the really "native" restaurants close to downtown and walking distance from our first house. The front end was a small grocery store, the middle was a restaurant with picnic tables and oil cloth tablecloths. The back end of the house was their home. Mama M was the cook, Papa was the maitre d' and cashier and the kids all did the waitering and kitchen help. We inhaled the enchiladas, tacos, all prepared to include Mama M's hand made tortillas. The beans were so delicious and I am sure they were cooked in lard. They served a dish which I called "colache". It was made with fresh chopped zucchini and hand cut corn from the cob all cooked by sauteing in butter. I make it to this day to the delight of my family. Yum! Yum!

If that didn't make your mouth water, I give up!

—⧖—

I will touch briefly on the political issues. With our current political climate continually heating up, I find myself remembering election times in Tucumcari. The different racial factors certainly contributed to an underlying mistrust. The division was along lines of heritage. Some of the families with direct ties to the descendants of the Spanish conquistadores felt superior and were usually held in high esteem in the community. Their ancestors had, in most case, been given large land grants by the Spanish government, which they had lost, sold or had

had reduced over the decades. The majority of the Hispanic speaking people were descendants of the 'Mestiza", the native Indian people. They mostly made up the laboring class or "middle management" population. When it came time for election, one of our honored citizens who was married to a local doctor and pulled a lot of weight in the community, decided who it was she wanted elected. She would drive her big, fancy car "across the tracks", pick up people that she then would transport to the polls. She paid each one she brought a certain amount on the proviso that the "x" on their ballots went in the square she told them. She spoke very little Spanish and some of them had no English, but pointing to the spot on the ballet was no problem. It was a know fact that in New Mexico, some ballot boxes in various counties disappeared for weeks in order to fill out ballots for people who now resided in the cemetery !!! Needless to say, she also wanted Jim to run things in the church the way SHE wanted, or she would remove her financial support. Jim knuckled under once or twice on some minor issues, but soon realizing what was happening, refused to comply and the support was withdrawn. Strange to say, a new family came into town, joined the church and pledged more than what her money had provided. Ah, yes! There is a God!! I served as an election monitor on one occasion and was amazed at the number of Anglo people who wanted to go in to the ballot booth to "help" their friends with their voting. I was a real hard nose and didn't allow it, but I'm sure there were many who did. That made me about as popular as a blister!

Once on a trip to Washington D.C., we contacted the Senator from Tucumcari. He had been a rather "disconnected" member of our church, but a fine moral upstanding member of the community. He used his church connection in his politicking and was easily elected to his position and went off to D.C. as a Senator Elect. We were allowed to sit in on a hearing about the road construction scandal in New Mexico. The roads which were only a very few years old were falling apart and the contractor who had won the bid and done the work was on the carpet! The most impressive evidence of the graft were copies of the checks (in the millions) that had been written to his wife for "esthetic consultation". As I sat in the balcony at the Senate hearings, I found myself feeling embarrassment for my town and state.

—◦◦◦—

When we first moved to Tucumcari, I thought it would be neighborly to visit everyone who lived close to us and get acquainted. My first choice was the lady across the street who lived in a very big, two story clapboard house, in much need of repair. It had been divided right down the middle and she lived in the right side, renting out the other side. She was a bit shocked to find she had company on her front stoop, but she invited me into a very long, narrow parlor with walls covered in various pictures. She perched tentatively on the edge of a velvet love seat and motioned me into a chair opposite. We rambled on for a while talking about families when I noticed that she was becoming quite ill at ease. In discussing family, she then asked me about my husband. She had heard that he smoked and remarked that she disapproved. She was appalled and waxed eloquent about "The devil's tools". I said yes (knowing he was a human being long before he became a minister). She shortly got up and excused herself. I watched her go around the corner in the kitchen and pick up her can and spit quite heartily into it. She was a tobacco chewer! Of course, she didn't know I had seen her. When she came back and sat down, I was really running out of conversation, so I began remarking about the pictures on the wall. One really interested me as I saw it as a conversation topic. It was a picture of a baby with its eyes closed. I asked her about it and she told me it was the only baby she had born, and that in the picture, it was dead!

Her sister lived right next door in a very small, cabin-like adobe house. We soon found out that she could stand behind the open front door, and look into a long mirror on the wall and watch everything that went on in our house and front yard. Sure made us cautious. My cousin Bernie and her delightful Italian husband Sam came to visit one summer and as they went out the front door to leave, I told them about this little lady and her habits. When we got as far as the sidewalk, Sam grabbed me, dipped me backwards in a clutching motion and gave me a kiss like you saw in the movies! He stood up triumphantly and said "There, that'll give her something to talk about!".

Ruth Ann's best friend was the daughter of our local New Mexico State policeman. She came over one day to play and Ruthi begged me to let Clara stay for dinner. I always overcooked and had enough to feed the local constabulary, so I of course said "yes". Clara's mother had no problem with her staying so we had a guest for dinner. The next day, her mother called, so embarrassed. She said, "This will give you some idea of how I keep house. Clara came home and said that the Froede's were so poor that they used pieces of cloth for napkins".

Traffic was pretty calm, although we had our chronic transgressors. Believe me, after living in Beverly Hills, anything having to do with traffic was tame by comparison. Cars were slightly different, lots of pickup trucks. Nobody owned a Mercedes and Cadillac was a type of grain feed. Mr. B did have a big Lincoln Continental that he took across the prairies regularly to see about his herd. He also would drive with one arm on the top of the adjacent seat and play with his kids while tooling along at 80-90. But he also would shave while we were flying in his single engine Cessna.

On one of my first ventures in my car around town, I came to an immediate screeching halt when I saw a driverless car coming toward me. It managed to stay in its lane and continue to move. I raced into the grocery store and poured out my concern about a near miss only to be told that that was just Bessie Bonnie Foyle. She had flaming red hair (bottle red, I am sure) and was only about five feet tall. She just never bothered to sit on anything that might bring her head up to the level of the dashboard. I guess she navigated her car by looking at the trees overhead (or maybe by the sun, the moon and stars).

Mr. B was a highly educated man with degrees from two different Universities, but his deepest love was ranching. He had the three ranches that he and his four sons maintained. He was married to a lovely, highly educated woman and also had one daughter. On occasional Sundays after church he would announce "Let's all go to Sands-Dorsey and get a sodie water". My family was delighted and off we would go. One day, as we were invited to the ranch for lunch, Mr. B drove us in his big car. When we were near the ranch, suddenly he braked, throwing us all around, drove off the road and headed over the prairie with us bounding in free flight over the bumps. "There's a heifer in trouble over there" he proclaimed as he drove one handed. Sure enough, there was a cow giving birth with much difficulty. We sat in the car rather stunned while he and the boys proceeded to get that calf born. When that was settled, we headed for the ranch house were Jim was meeting us. We didn't realize that this was a day the workers had decided to brand and castrate the latest "crop" of calves. We sat in the bleachers at their arena to watch, but Mr. B yelled out to Jim to come help as they had a rather reluctant young male on their hands. We had just saved enough money to buy Jim a new suit, which unfortunately he had chosen to wear that particular day. Jim went forward to help and needless to say, the suit was ruined—but—the calf was branded and castrated, much to Mr. B's pleasure.

As soon as I spotted Mr. B in his double breasted suit, fresh haircut and manure sprinkled boots, I knew we were going to be doing something special. Remember, this is a man with two master's degrees from two different universities. He had told us to make arrangements to be away for a day or so and we had done that. Kids were taken care of, dog was settled and off we went. With Mrs. B in tow, we headed for the local airport (a tiny field at best). We were loaded into his single engine plane which he used to check on his various ranches over the Southwest. I have a deep seated fear of flying, due to many close calls in my past and it was running rampant over me because of "small plane terror". Who can back out at that point? The motor gunned and we were off like a herd of turtles, into the glorious blue sky with me clutching anything close and clutchable! We were told that we were going to Denver as Mr. B was going to take us to a livestock sale. What a thrill!! Anyway, it certainly would be a new experience for both Jim and I. During the flight Mr. B remarked that he hadn't had time to shave and he promptly pulled out a battery run shaver, took both hands off the wheel and proceeded to shave. At that point I almost lost my eyeballs as I watched and prayed he had a light beard. Suddenly, as we crossed over into Colorado, he asked if we had ever seen the Air Force Academy. We both said "no", so we did a quick 180 and he headed for the campus. Next thing we know, he flew up the side of the chapel, straight up and around!! Not once but twice. I had practically passed out by then and was amazed that the Blue Angels weren't hot on our tail to arrest us. When we finally landed and got into our rental car, we headed for the massive stock yards of Denver where we wandered around on planks between various pens of different kinds of cattle and sheep and their inevitable by-product. We settled into the stands to watch the proceedings which were like the ones we see and enjoy even now at the L.A. County Fair. After enough animals had been paraded to his satisfaction, we were finished and he made his purchases. Then Mr. B waxed eloquent about the Brown Hotel which apparently was the crown hotel of Colorado. He decided we were going to eat there. We walked into the lobby gazing goggle eyed at the high ceilinged room we were in. Mr.B walked up to a porter and said "beautiful place you got here". Being the snob that I was, I shrunk back behind Jim and we trudged on to the dining room. The maitre d' looked us over and headed to the furthest table where we sat next to the swinging kitchen doors. After perusing the menu, Mr. B asked the waiter "Do you serve lamb?—I raise sheep". I think the waiter had already guessed that. Indeed, it was a delightful lunch and believe it or not, the trip home was so uneventful that it has faded away from my memory. We must have arrived home safely, because, as you see, I am here to tell the story.

My oldest son Rick, tells the story of going with his dad and Mr. B to a local clothing store that specialized in cowboy gear. After some shopping, Mr. B chose the most expensive Stetson in the store, tried it on for size and proceeded to buy it. They headed for the ranch to have some lunch, but before they went in the house, Mr. B lead them to one of the pastures that was filledwith cattle. He threw the hat into the dirtiest part of the corral, whistled and stomped until the cattle were trampling over the hat to his satisfaction. Climbed over the fence and retrieved the hat, dusted it off and pushed it back into shape, made the crease, clapped it on his head and said "Now it's broke in".

One trip to the lake, Jim and I had gone with Mr. B and his family, helping to launch his new cabin cruiser. We then took off for a day of water skiing. By mid afternoon, I had finished my allotted time and Jim's turn came. He was having a wonderful time when we could see a storm forming over the cliffs. Within a few minutes it hit and the waves on this narrow lake were running three to four feet high, tossing the boat around like a cork. Jim wanted to get off the skis and into the boat RIGHT NOW! Every time he approached the prow of the boat, a wave would hit and lift the boat up several feet in the air, then slam it down to the water, missing Jim by a whisker. We finally worked him back to the stern where we were able to pull him out of the water. He was exhausted by all the effort. Suddenly, the motor conked out and we were tossed around like matchsticks. Mr. B said we needed to swim to shore, which we did, scared and shivering. Like the good captain, he stayed on board while the boat headed for the rocks and concrete of the dam and proceeded to smash to smithereens. He fortunately had deserted just before that happened. We sat on the shoreline and watched. As I think back on it, Mr. B with his beautiful spirit of adventure, just laughed and said he was glad we were all safe and "that's the way things go!" Mr. B replaced his boat, but I also think back and realize that we never went out on the boat with Mr. B again.

—⁕—

Long Gone Motels—Route 66

Historic Route 66 Motel

Owning and operating a motel in Tucumcari in the 50's and 60's was a surefire bet for success. Leaving Albuquerque, driving 100+ miles, racing off the Llano Estacada and coming into the bowl that was our county, you were in motel heaven. The still famous Route 66 threaded its way through the city and set its sights for Amarillo, 120 miles to the east. Many, many people say they have "GONE THROUGH Tucumcari". Few have stopped. A family from our church owned the Cactus Motel. It was situated on a very large piece of property, the first motel on the western end of the highway. The front house was large and the family lived there with cabins extending behind the house to the furthest back end of the lot. Mrs. W was very faithful about bringing the four younger children to church and dropping them off but I think Mr. W kept the older boy at home to help maintain the property as I only remember seeing them on rare occasions. It was not a Best Western, but it was clean, functional and had good rates. Patty was my daughter Ruthi's age and they were like sisters, so we saw a lot of her. Three younger brothers were stair steps with about one year age between them. Their names were Rodney, Randy and Ricky. The way I got to know them was through the children's choir. There were a lot of kindergarten through 6th grade kids in church and I thought they could be a magnet for getting the parents involved, so I started a children's choir.

Children's Choir—Circa 1959

We ended up with about 20 regulars and they performed for a number of church occasions, swelling the ranks in the pews by many adult parents. I made robes for each of them out of white fabric and attached large red bows to the neck. They were quite a sight to behold. The most memorable performance we did was at the annual Christmas pageant where we sang all the good, appropriate Christmas songs. Rodney and Randy were in the front row as they were the smallest and even looked like twins. Randy was very cross-eyed, wore glasses and was somber while Rodney was the happy one, always with a big smile. This particular performance, Randy had worn his new cowboy boots which were great, but he had put them on the wrong feet. Also, Rodney rocked forward and back in time to the music while Randy rocked side to side. Therefore, Randy's boots were a fascination as the toes pointed out and up and rocked even more. As usual, the audience ended up laughing through most of the performance. Such a pleasant memory.

—⟋⟍—

The First Baptist Church was just a few blocks from our First Presbyterian Church and we had come to know John and Ruth, the pastor and his wife as good friends, Ruth being one of my best friends. It was an "unwritten law" that pastor's wives could not be "good friends" with anyone in their own church, so Ruth and I became instant buddies. The first Baptist Church was the "mother" church with a large number of "splinter" churches in the community, probably formed over conflicts of theological differences.

A gentleman known to be one of the local "reprobates", well known in the community for public drunkenness and general misbehavior, came to Jim and said he had found Christ and wanted to be baptized. Jim was floored, but immediately agreed to do it the following Sunday morning. Well, Frank wasn't about to settle for anything as mundane as being "sprinkled". He wanted to be IMMERSED. Jim called John, explained the situation and asked if we could use their baptistry. John was most agreeable and a date was set. I need to explain the architecture of the Baptist church. The sanctuary was very large with a front wall probably two to three stories high. The wall was blank except for a very large frame surrounding the inset baptistry centered on the wall, looking like a picture window. All the interested parties had gathered in the pews awaiting the coming event. Soon Jim and Frank appeared, dressed in white robes which concealed Jim's waist high waders. The service proceeded and finally got to the point of immersion, whereupon, Jim took hold of Frank's nose and bent him back to dip him. Well, Frank must have had an epiphany, because he lurched backwards, pulling Jim under with him, immediately filling his waders with water up to his chest!! They both came up sputtering, staggering and thrashing around while we all watched, stunned! They finally got their bearings and were able to climb out, both looking like drowned rats. Imagine trying to move with waders filled with water. To the day of his death, Jim would tell this story and proudly claim the fact that he had not only been "sprinkled" as a child, but had been "immersed" as an adult.

Related somewhat to that story is the one about Mrs. W who was one of the local florists. She was a lovely, congenial woman and often had requests for church flowers. She also was extremely obese and to top it off was quite short. This one particular request required her to decorate the altar section of one of the local churches for an upcoming wedding. She proceeded to bring in all her flowers and to work behind the screen that covered the baptistry which was located in the floor of the nave. As she worked, she stepped backwards to get a better perspective, lost her balance and fell into the water. At this point a funeral procession came walking into the church and, because her struggles to free herself from the water would be noisy, to say the least, she realized that she couldn't continue to struggle, so she laid quietly in the water until the funeral service had been completed. After all was said and done, a few ushers were finally able to extricate her, much to her embarrassment.

Funerals in Tucumcari often took on the air of a Roman orgy, without the sex angle. There were two prominent morticians in town, one Caucasian (or "anglo" as we were called) and one Hispanic. They were occasionally spotted racing out to Gaynell Avenue (Route 66) where they would try to be the first ones there and ended up arguing who was going to get the bodies resulting from the frequent accidents. Though we had little opportunity to participate in the Hispanic community activities, we were present at one of their funerals, presided over by one of the Mr. D's. We were rather shocked when the funeral director invited people to come forward to kiss the corpse or even climb into the casket with the occupant. A few people did just that. This wasn't a practice that we encouraged Jim to adopt.

During a recent concert performance, I was put in mind of an occasion where one of our famous old cowboys had died. Jim was asked to conduct the service and therefore it was held in our church. The family, wanting to do something special, asked me to get a quartet together and sing. We did, choking up and with tears in our eyes. Their request was "Streets of Laredo" with lyrics about the "young cowboy wrapped up in white linen—as cold as the grave". Gratifying to be a part of a tribute to an old cowboy.

—⚜—

The most colorful character that became embroiled in our life in Tucumcari was Father Ray. He was the priest at the local Roman Catholic church. It enjoyed a very large congregation, 1000-2000 souls, where we boasted only a few hundred! Ray had spent almost all of his adult life in China as a Maryknoll priest. He first served in a Chinese community with a large number of nuns, until the Japanese came into power which resulted in their incarceration for over two years in a barbaric prison camp. His health was seriously jeopardized and he was finally released. He returned to his mission station, but was soon confronted by the Chinese communists who had invaded and again was incarcerated where his health really broke. When he was finally released, he was assigned to the job of being a "spy" for the church. This entailed taking on a civilian posture (his passport listed his occupation as "writer") and going into "iron curtain" countries to find out the level of Christian activity and the ability of the churches to continue to exist under communist regimes. This information was forwarded directly to the Vatican. After a couple of years of harrowing work, he returned to the states and was assigned the position of head pastor of the Tucumcari church where we were privileged to know him. Our first dinner in the rectory was a veritable banquet! His Hispanic cook prepared exotic soups, lobster, and elegant desserts. We were surprised to find that Ray had chosen a different wine for EACH course. Well, not being drinkers, I imagine by dessert, I was ready to dance on the table! His den was where he relaxed with reading, music and TV. His brother was an executive with a record company, so one corner of the room was stacked high with record albums. Another corner of the room was stacked with a variety of cases of wines. When I asked Ray about that, he explained that he was required at mass to finish the wine that had been consecrated for the service and that some days he "felt like Chablis and some days, Chardonnay". All new knowledge for me as I didn't know about trans-substantiation (wine to blood) theory of the Catholic church.

After we left Tucumcari, we did learn that he had been assigned by the church to resume his clandestine role as a "spy" and was sent to Ghana. We finally heard from him that he was planning to retire to San Diego to live with his sister, which delighted us as we would be geographically near to him. One day, we received a phone call from his sister informing us that he had been murdered in Ghana. He had gone for his usual morning trip to the beach to swim and was found face down in the sand, dead with all his possessions missing. What a shock. His sister pursued our government and the government of Ghana to have the situation investigated, but in spite of all her efforts, because she was elderly and had no more money for this, she finally let it go and nothing other than "vandalism" was determined. One of my fondest memories of Ray was the story he told of losing his mother at age 12. He became "the mother" of the family and declared that he had had all of domesticity that he ever could desire. Being from a strong Irish background, he happily went into the priesthood at an early age. A flattering remark he also frequently made was—that I, Mary, was the best argument <u>against</u> celibacy that he had ever known! What a boost to the ego.

Our neighbor across the street and down at the corner was a woman with two children, one boy and one girl. The boy was about the same age as my oldest son, nine years old. When I mentioned that these children were playing at our house, some of the church people became upset and informed me that the mother had the reputation of being one of the town's "ladies of the evening". Needless to say, I was shocked, but even more so when I discovered that both children were loaded with head lice. I thought the best thing to do was to tell the mother. I went over to their house and was greeted by a rather unkempt, young, but bitter looking woman with a very hostile attitude. She grudgingly did invite me in. I was as gracious as possible in explaining her children's condition. She accepted what I said and indicated that she had been shampooing their hair but having no success. I told her I would be happy to get some medication for her, which I did. I also bought a very fine tooth comb and after applying the medication, we combed their hair to clean it up and get rid of the invaders. We did this a number of times and they were cured!

I had no particular contact with her until after we had moved to the new manse a few months later. One day, there was a knock at my door and I went to see who it was. There stood a very plain, clean, neatly dressed woman with hair pulled into a bun at the back of her neck, holding a basket. She looked very familiar, but I drew a blank. She said "Hi, remember me—Ellen?" I was flabbergasted, invited her in and we had a lovely talk. Her purpose in visiting me was to sell me home made bread. Her church was raising money to build a building and she had offered the talent of bread baking as her contribution. Come to find out that after we had cured her children and occasionally greeted each other on the street, she had joined one of the small Pentecostal churches in town. She had an incredible conversion experience and was now very active in their community. She continued to sell me bread each week until we left town. I regret to say, that in my busy life, I never followed through and often wonder what happened to the family.

Another of the prominent families in Tucumcari were members of our church. The mother Rose and her husband Gary were transplants from Texas. Gary, who had been a cowboy and ranch owner, owned and operated the local stockyard with the purpose of fattening the cattle preparing them for shipment to the big city for sale or for slaughter. In order to increase the "bottom line" of profit, they also dried, bagged and sold the manure to the local farmers. One day Gary and his son Barry had worked all day bagging their treasures for sale. When they returned home, Rose stopped them at the door, examined their boots and said "Don't come in—you smell bad". Gary's reply was "That smells like MONEY!"

Gary was never one to waste anything. Hides were sold and he periodically came home with a big plastic bag of a delicacy known by the locals as "calf fries". Jim's mother was visiting us from Washington D.C. and we had decided to have a special dinner at the new Ramada Inn. Nana was always the absolute perfect picture of female gentility and after we had browsed the menu, she ordered the "rocky mountain oysters". Jim and I were stunned and he leaned over to explain to her as delicately as possible that they were "calf fries" or bull's testicles. She only expressed disappointment and disbelief because she exclaimed how she did love oysters . . . and went on to order the frog's legs.

We were so pleased that Rose, who had a lovely alto voice, sang with us in the choir. Because it was August, the choir was on hiatus and Jackie, our organist/choir director had assembled a quartet to sing on Sunday. We were to meet at Jackie's house at 7 P.M. Thursday evening to rehearse. 7:00 arrived, 7:15, 7:30 and NO ROSE! Suddenly, the doorbell rang and a slightly harried Rose appeared. As she stood next to me to rehearse, it was obvious that she had had a drink before coming, probably accounting for her late arrival. The song chosen for us to sing was "Breathe on me".

Their daughter Elaine was about twelve years old when they arrived in town with her "drop dead" gorgeous younger brother Barry. She was one of the homeliest girls I had ever seen with straggly flaming red hair and scrawny body to match. She took a lot of teasing and we always felt sorry for her as her mother was such a stunningly beautiful woman. Just a few years later, after we had left town and returned for a visit, here was this movie star quality young lady who literally took our breath away. Hans Christian Anderson knew what he was doing when he wrote "The Ugly Duckling".

While I was substitute teaching music in the two grade schools, Rose was a full time teacher. One day, as we ate lunch together, the principal came in with a shocked look on her face. She came to our table and sat down to tell Rose that Gary had dropped dead at the stockyard. He was in his mid 40's! What a tragedy. Eventually the family left and went back to Fort Stockton, Texas.

—ɯ—

An aside here . . . remembering the substitute teaching. I am not a teacher. Nor am I a good piano player, but Mr. B thought differently. He knew I could sing. Among many other civic responsibilities, he was serving as president of the school board. When he was faced with the problem of replacing the music teacher for the two grade schools, he was stumped. The current teacher was expecting her first baby and had been put on bed rest for the remainder of her pregnancy. I was shocked to receive his phone call asking if I would take over the position for the six months remaining in the school year. Sensing his desperate manner, I finally agreed to do so.

My students were still young enough to enjoy all sorts of items to make music, or create rhythm other than the piano. In order to handle a job I had no experience in, I came up with the idea of using, first of all, a Walt Disney record from my children's collection called "A toot, a whistle, a plunk and a boom" which dealt with instruments reminiscent of pre-historic musical instruments. The younger grades had a ball!! And surprisingly, the older children got a kick out of it, as we used very basic instruments to provide the proper sounds. We even gave an occasional impromptu "concert" showing off our remarkable skills. For the last part of the school year, I used a record album of a number of the classical composers which featured one perfect example of their style for each of the famous composers—Bach, Beethoven, etc. We listened to the music and learned about the life of each man. How delighted I was to be approached on the street one day by one of the mothers who expressed her amazement over learning all this musical information from her son. Some of the fifth and sixth grade boys were fully man sized. They also smelled like horses. When I was faced with one particularly unruly boy, I couldn't make him sit up straight, so, much to the amusement of the class, I made him sit with a yard stick down his back until class ended.

The last month of the school year usually had temperatures in the 100-110 degree range. Typical for late spring in New Mexico. In order to manage "the troops" with no air conditioning, I borrowed the Camp Song Books from the church and we had a raucous month of camp song singing. It turned out to be lots of fun, even for the 18 year old ranch boys who had been held over, grade after grade! On the last day, I had placed a sheet of paper, face down on each desk and told the children not to turn it over until I said so. When they were finally all seated, groaning and bellyaching thinking I was springing a test on them, I told them to turn the paper over. I had typed "THANK YOU FOR BEING MY CLASS AND HAVE A WONDERFUL SUMMER".

One very warm day, as I was leaving the school, I saw a cloud of dust near one of the storage sheds. When I went to investigate it, I found two girls, rolling around on the ground, clutching each other's hair, clawing and biting. I was stunned as a good size crowd had gathered to watch and cheer on their various dervishes. Something possessed me and I marched into the fray, pointed my finger at each and every one and yelled at them to get off the school grounds, grabbed one of the girls by the arm and hauled her off to the side. Then I banished both of them and told them to go home. Well, when the dust finally settled and I was alone, slightly unkempt and out of breath, the reality of my madness set in and I shook all the way to the car. I have no idea where that courage came from. Thank God, I didn't have to ever experience it again. So ended my career as a public school teacher.

Sports were important in town. Football, of course, was a carryover from all of the people who had emigrated from Texas. I loved going to the high school games in the fall of the year. When Rick was thirteen, he decided he wanted to play football. He was not very tall and had a thin, but strong physique. When he lined up with all of the ranch and farm boys, he looked somewhat like a midget, but he was determined. Jim and I decided to go to watch on the day they were picking the team players. We spotted Rick right away, except that he looked like he had put on a hundred pounds with the donning of the issued uniform. The helmut was too large and he looked more like the football dummy used for practice, a real bobblehead. As he wobbled over to us, we could see the oversized pads in the front of his trousers were so much too large that they rotated and flopped between his legs until they finally knocked him down. While stifling our giggles, we tried stabilizing the pads so that he could manage a play or two, but to no avail. His decision to quit became final when a two hundred pound tackle landed squarely on top of him and convinced him that his Olympic dreams were over. He did go on with his swimming and diving and took lots of medals in that field when we moved to Texas.

Jim, on the other hand had never wanted to play football. He decided now to help out by coaching the second string team for the "pre-game" games. This also required that he referee the second team games. He proudly donned his black and white striped shirt and stepped into the fray with the whistle in his mouth, the yellow hanky in his pocket and a heart that was beating wildly in his chest. One particular game was a close one against a nearby town who had sent their championship team to play against ours. The fans in the audience got really upset by some of the decisions that were made by the referees and the booing started. Primarily directed at Jim. Here was this "Godly" pastor making decisions that effected the outcome of their game and they were unhappy. He heard a lot about it as he went around the town following that game.

One time, he recounted to us at home, that during the game a ball came flying through the air and could have resulted in a touchdown run if caught by our losing team. He was standing at the sidelines as it headed straight toward him. He said he had the almost uncontrollable desire to grab that ball and head for the goal line to make the winning points. Fortunately, the feeling passed and he let the ball fly beyond the stands.

How well I remember going to one of the out of town games in late October. We knew it would be cold so we dressed accordingly. I had layered everything I owned to the point where I could hardly move. Jim was to act as "spotter" for his friend who was broadcasting the game. Hurrah! I would be in the broadcasting booth with him, but was stunned to find out that it was not heated. Shortly after the start of the game, a few flakes of snow drifted down. Then more and more . . . By then, the opposing team's fans were down to about twelve and I think that we were the only ones from out of town, so our side of the stands was completely empty as the band had retreated to the buses and gone on their merry way home. The opposing band tried to play for a few minutes, but by then, they were wading through many drifts of snow. The game actually went on to the bitter end, to the point that we could hardly see the players on the field. When we finally finished and started home, it took us hours to get there because of all the snow that been dumped by the blizzard. Strange, but I can't remember who of if anyone won that game. I've blocked it all.

—⚌—

Escaping from Hungary was a life saving experience for Mike's family. Mike's career in his homeland was as a policeman with the secret service in Budapest. Because it was so painful for them to speak of all of this, the rest of this story is piecemeal from years of conversations I had with them. Having survived World War II and the Nazi occupation, they then were subjected to the communist regime sweeping through Europe. A good friend warned them of the upcoming Russian invasion and the probability of them being arrested or killed. He and his young wife, Mary, had just time enough to pack a bag in the night and escape through the back door. This required fording a stream and they headed for the railroad station. Both were soaked and this was wintertime. They were able to get on a train heading out of Hungary. While on the train (apparently a long period of time) Mary, newly pregnant, became seriously ill and was pretty much semi-comatose for the trip. When they eventually arrived in Austria, they were sent to a displaced person's camp. The only belongings they had were in the suitcase. They finally reached a "displaced person's" camp and Mary had the baby, Editka (Edith) and dressed her in the few petticoats she had managed to save as they had no other clothing and very little money.

Being devout Catholics and wanting to come to America, they applied for DP reassignment. The Catholic church at Tucumcari apparently had requested a DP so they were brought there as janitors for the church. This was not while our priest friend Ray was there. The only information I have about their experience was that it was not good. Mike somehow got in touch with the pastor who had preceded Jim at the Presbyterian Church, left the Catholic situation and became janitor at our church. When we arrived in town, they were well established in the community and Edith was a teenager. Mike was a joy and a tireless worker. In addition to the church work, he managed to get many other jobs in the community and they soon owned their own home.

Mary was a pleasure to be with! She was a beautiful woman with a delightful sense of humor. Also an incredible cook. Her "offerings" at group functions and pot luck suppers were always looked forward to. One of the tasks she performed was to prepare all of the elements for communion. One story tells of her first time doing that. Mary, with her culinary skills made her own wine from fruit that they grew in their backyard garden. Imagine the surprise of the congregants when they lifted their communion glasses, downed the liquid and began choking on this lovely homemade WINE. Of course, the good fathers made them aware of the fact the we Presbyterians used grape juice! (Which incidentally was perpetrated by the Welch family in order to promote more use of their product).

It was 7:00 P.M. and Mary hadn't yet appeared for Circle meeting. We knew that she was always present, so we were concerned. She suddenly burst into the room, hair flying and red faced. "I've just been attacked by Jello Yackets!!" Well, of course we immediately were convulsed with laughter realizing that she was talking about bees, but her accent took over. Naturally, we came around to the reality and treated her for her being a victim and in pain.

Edith, their lovely daughter was our teenage babysitter. How fortunate we were to have her. She was such a beautiful and loving girl and very popular in the community. One summer evening, she was babysitting and apparently had a friend who came to see her. They stood at the door and talked for quite a long time, I would guess, because when we got home and she left, we walked in to the house and saw that the ceiling was completely covered by dark, grey moths!! Well, Jim said he would get the fly swatter and I stopped him saying that one swat and they would all fly! We then got the brilliant idea of sucking them up in the Electrolux, one by one. Many vacuum bags later we had succeeded in sucking them all up and disposed of the bags.

Over the years I heard that Edith had entered the Miss New Mexico beauty pageant to participate. After finishing her schooling, she married and had children, but when we visited Tucumcari two years ago and spent time with a very aged, ill Mike, found out that she had died of breast cancer at 55 years of age. We visited her grave in great sorrow.

Mary had also died many years before and Mike had connected with an Hungarian woman who he married and who was lovingly caring for him in his final years. Though he was very debilitated when we saw him, he looked at my daughter and spoke her name "Ruthi". We dissolved in tears and were overcome with memories of her following Mike around the church premises.

—m—

In the parlance of the Paris Hiltons and Nicole Richies of today, I must talk about my BFF (meaning Best Friends Forever.) In Tucumcari, my BFF was Ruth W. She was the wife of the local pastor at the First Baptist Church whose baptistry we had used. I emphasize FIRST because, for such a small town, we were overwhelmed with churches, most of which were offshoots of the Baptist church. Seems like every time there was some disagreement, a group would pick up their toys and go off and start a new church. Fortunately, that had never happened to the Presbyterians. I do remember one day that Jim came home saying that he had been reading the church session meeting notes and had discovered an incident from 50 or more years previous that the session had excommunicated one of the people for "behavior not befitting a church member". But I digress.

Now, with that departure, let me tell you about my BFF, Ruth W. She was a bit younger than I was, but we had children similar in age. I got a call from her one day saying that AT & T was changing the telephone system in New Mexico, from operator assisted to dial. When Lily Tomlin does her "ringy-dingy" routine, I am reminded of Tucumcari and their antiquated phone system of cords and a huge board. Ruth, through some church connection, had been given the job of training the 5,000 or so residents of the county in the new system and she wanted me to join her in this adventure. I was delighted as my minor in college had been speech and drama. We were given a car, a huge reel to reel projector, sample dial telephones and cases of information flyers. We mapped out the city and decided the best way to do this was to start in the schools, which we took a few months to do. The routine was to greet the audience, explain what we were doing and then show a short film on the whole process. We did this one classroom at a time with an opportunity at the end of the presentation for the viewers to experiment with the new dial system on the dummy phones. We were always well received if for no reason other than relief for the kids from the boredom of classroom activity. When it came to the adults, you had another story. Many of them just couldn't get the hang of it and they voiced sincere complaints about having to change. They knew the operators by name and some of the calls they made were to people with a two digit phone number, easy to remember. We spent many more hours teaching them as individuals. After completing the schools, we pretty much went by church and community groups, which comprised most of the community. Then on to the nursing homes, which really was a challenge. Shut-ins presented problems as we approached them as individuals. Hearing problems were solved by making the company aware of the situation and then providing special equipment. This whole adventure took us a number of months, but by the time we were finished, we were disappointed that it was over. The whole experience provided me with a close friend and we enjoyed many lunches, shared babysitting and just "hung out". I was broken hearted when Ruth, John and family moved to Brownsville, Texas where they served a large church. John died shortly thereafter, a very young man and Ruth went back to live with her family. We just lost touch. To this day I still value the friendship we had. In the "today talk" amongst the famous—BFF should be BFF-T Best Friends Forever, TEMPORARILY.

Having been carefully schooled in my "previous life" as a working wife and mother at seminary, I remembered what they had told us about NOT developing close friendships within the church. To demonstrate that, one Sunday as I walked in for worship service, I noticed a lady I hadn't seen in a while, so I approached her and wanted to know how she was. I stood for a few minutes talking and then went to my own seat. After the service, another lady came up to me and said "You didn't bother to greet ME this morning". I solved the problem in each church by singing in the choir! I was lucky in that the community welcomed me with open arms—the new kid on the block—and I had a close circle of friends that encompassed churches other than ours and was able to enjoy their fellowship outside our church. I felt free to just be myself with no fear of criticism from fellow churchgoers. As I said previously about Jim, "I was a human being long before I became a minister's wife".

—⚬⚬—

Ted was well ensconced in Tucumcari by the time we arrived. He was a young, single man from a small town in Iowa, had his degree in music, and was the music teacher in the high school. He was a much loved choir director at our church and we enjoyed our Thursday night rehearsals and subsequent performances on Sunday. One year as the holidays were just around the corner, Ted decided he would conduct a community "Messiah" for the churched and unchurched to enjoy. We had quite a good response from all the community including the AME church which had all black members. They had such good voices and contributed a lot to the venture. One particular evening, as we were practicing, Ted became visibly agitated. He started to scold us for the fact that we kept our music in our laps and our noses in the books. He had no eye contact with us whatsoever. At the end of his lecture, he shook his finger and announced "I want to see every blue eye looking up at me while we sing". This was greeted with gasps, dead silence and obvious discomfort on his part as it sunk in to him what he had just said. We did go on to perform for the whole community and it turned out to be a big success, though never repeated while we lived there. When Ted retired back to Iowa, he decided to spend a good deal of his time as a volunteer teacher in New Guinea. He adopted a young boy and supported him through all of his schooling and this year's Christmas card showed Maurice receiving his Doctorate degree. Such a sacrifice on Ted's part.

—⚬⚬—

Dan and Margie were transplants from the deep south. They had the delightful warm and rolling accents typical of the south. Superstitions influenced their day to day living, but they were devoted members of the church. Dan often did "scut" work around the church and Margie always was a presence in the church kitchen when we had "eating affairs". She was very active in the women's organizations. One day, Jim got up in the morning and went to work but was soon home sick enough with the flu and all its symptoms that he knew he would be unable to conduct the services on Sunday, which required that the elders take over. On the following Monday, he received a frantic call from Margie saying that she was also sick with the flu, but the thing that worried her most was that her best friend was also down with the same malady. As she phoned various friends, she found many of them also down. They had put their heads together and came to the conclusion that "the Russians were flying at high altitude and dropping flu pellets on them". After Jim recovered from stifling his laughter, he remarked "and they only affect the Presbyterians?" That, we hoped was the end of that.

Penny and Stanley substituted as my surrogate "mom and dad". Penny was this tall, overweight, loving woman who at the age of 55 had taken up painting. Her work was so remarkable and I still have two of her very large oil paintings in my home. I think of Penny each time I look at them. Stanley was a "business only" kind of guy and could always be counted on to do repairs and general upkeep at the church and our manse. He had been a railroad man for his whole career, energetic and unwilling to retire to idleness.

Penny taught the kindergarten Sunday school class and was a charmer. One Easter, she decided to have the children plant flowers to take home. Each child was given a small pot, a little handful of flower seeds and told to plant them in the holes she had dug in the soil of each pot. When they were done, she patted the soil over the seeds and said "Now what do we say?" One little boy raised his hand and then proceeded to pat the soil and said he would repeat what his mother always said. The next statement, as he patted was "Now, by God, grow!"

—⚏—

Tallest Building in Town
Quay County Courthouse

Growing up, girl scouting was a real thrill for me as my mother would drive me into town to go to the meetings that were held in the city hall. Our town only had the one troop. I loved earning the merit badges that Mother sewed on my sash. After nosing around in Tucumcari for a while, I found out that there was a girl scout troop that met in the First Baptist Church. Well, I decided that there were not that many girls in town and it would be nice to have a community group. After meeting with the various people involved, I volunteered to lead the group. We ended up going from location to location in order to accommodate the growing organization. I complained one day to Mr. B about the difficulties of transporting our belongings week to week. He said he would talk to the contractor that he had used to build the manse and see what could be done. I was soon contacted by Tom, the contractor. He said he had a small piece of property that he would donate and we proceeded to gather a minimal amount of money to pay him. The building plans moved forward. Just three blocks from the manse. There were even a few trees on the property. The building was built with cement blocks and had two rooms and a bathroom. Each room was probably only about 15 x 15, but big enough for us to create a craft center and a meeting table to work on with chairs along the sides. The whole community ended up donating things that we could use and we settled in a bona fide girl scout troop with a rousing open house to dedicate the property.

We met periodically through the week and some of the mothers helped with the merit badge work. Having been an office nurse before marrying, I got the idea that the hospital could use some candy stripers with our dedicated girl scouts to start the plan. The hospital had no volunteers at that point, so they were excited about the possibility. Each "shift" of girls was accompanied by one of the mothers. I made pink and white striped seersucker pinafores for each girl and even made them nurses caps to wear while they were on duty. The response was great and the program was in full swing when we moved, so I missed out on the opportunity to be fully involved with it. On one return visit, I found out that some of the mothers had taken up the challenge and had formed an adult volunteer group that was enjoying great success in the community.

—m—

The King family became very good friends of ours. Bill was the owner of our local newspaper and also the newspaper in another town. He was a part of a huge syndicated Newspaper conglomerate that ran businesses all over the country. His wife Clara was a housewife with a house full of girls, four to be exact. After we left town, we were delighted to know that they had had two boys to follow. Clara was a role model for me. She had been raised on a farm in Kansas with no running water or electricity and had a wonderful laid back personality that I, with my ADD, emulated as often as possible. They had built a very large ranch house out on one of the mesas. One day since she was planning to host a group of people from the church, I drove out to their house to help her get ready. When I arrived, Bill had gone to work, the girls had gone to school and all was quiet on the Western front. Bill was always the first one up in the morning, headed for the kitchen to make the coffee and start the morning meal while Clara slept in. It was always exactly the same . . . egg over easy, toast, fruit juice and milk. It never varied and I asked Clara about that "Don't the kids get bored with the same old, same old?" Her reply was that they had never had anything different so how could they know? To avoid boredom and the problem of wondering each morning what to fix, I had a schedule for breakfast as I was usually dragging myself into the kitchen to get food for the family. Monday . . . French toast. Tuesday . . . boiled eggs . . . You get the idea! Well, as soon as I had arrived, I expected to pitch in right away, but Clara insisted that we sit down and have a cup of tea as she wanted to watch her favorite TV show. I joined her in the living room and became a little nervous as I expected to help. She calmly said the dessert was made and in the frig, the girls had picked up their own rooms. Bill had put the dishes in the dishwasher. She would run the vacuum and maybe do a little dusting, but her view of entertaining was that if they were really her friends, it wouldn't matter to them what condition the house was in. What a freeing-up philosophy of life. I always slaved so hard when I knew company was coming that I usually resented the fact that they were there when they finally arrived!!

One Sunday, Bill had barbecued in the back yard, come in the house and they had all relaxed when a windstorm came up. Suddenly, they were aware that the barbecue had blown over and the grass caught on fire. It quickly spread as the prairies were usually very dry. The firefighters came out from town to no avail and the fire managed to destroy many acres of prairie grass. Some animals were killed and unfortunately, some law suits were a result of this accident. Fires were always a threat. I have kept in touch with the family all these years and when I visited them in Tucson a few years ago found Clara in the advanced stages of Parkinson's. She died last year and Bill has moved into a retirement home. Lovely family.

As is typical of small towns in those days and the fact that Tucumcari was stuck out in the middle of nowhere, the churches were very much the center of social activities, so we always had great social times with our members. Jim and I were particularly driven by the wonderful experiences we had as newlyweds sponsoring a huge youth group at Fremont Church in Sacramento. Now, in Tucumcari, every Sunday night, we gathered the kids in Fellowship Hall, fixed them dinner, and had them conduct a worship service. Then we would "play". We even had folk dancing which sometimes ended up being "line dancing"

similar to what you see adults doing nowadays. We became a social magnet for kids who had no church affiliations, but came because of "word of mouth" advertising.

As regards social gathering, the Presbyterians were known for their wonderful contributions of ample food for their meetings. Pot luck was a given and each contributor planned to outdo the next on quality and quantity of food. We had one couple though, who I am sure lived very frugally. We were always told to bring enough food for 12 people. They came with, for example, two chicken wings . . . two pieces of pie, etc. We always wondered what they would come up with for the party. Two doughnuts????

In order to convince everyone that we did not live in an abjectly primitive condition, I must tell you about the roller skating rink. There was a huge barn-like structure near the edge of town that had been "adopted" by a young couple and made into a rather sophisticated skating rink. Of course, the kids in town were drawn like steel to a magnet. Mine were no exception. Ricky was an athletic participant and did some fancy skating. Ruthi and her buddies formed a group that did square dancing on skates. There were two boys (our neighbors) and two girls, Ruthi and a friend. I made outfits for them, red checkered shirts for the guys to wear with jeans and jean-like short tutu skirts with ruffled checkered blouses for the girls. They performed many of the proscribed square dances that were popular with adults. The act caught on and we went all over the state with these kids performing their skills for particular group fund raisers. Now, I was a bored housewife at that time (not really) and convinced two of my neighbors that while the kids were in school, we should be taking advantage of the exercise involved in skating. We did just that and went many afternoons to practice with no intervention from the many skaters usually there. I really got good at it and loved spending the leisurely hours on skates. I could even squat down at full speed, lean over and pick up an object with my teeth!!! How about that for an old lady. We moved away and I haven't been on skates once since!!

Other evidence of our sophistication . . . a young man came to town and opened a photography business. Jim was walking down the street one day wearing a suit, a fancy multistriped necktie, a navy colored snap brim hat and a muted plaid overcoat. Suddenly, a fellow appeared before him introducing himself and asking Jim if he could photograph him. Jim thought that would be good fun, so he agreed. Mr. LeDeane (I am afraid I have forgotten his first name) took him into the studio and explained that he was experimenting with a new technicolor process. He had always worked in black and white with color added by his painting finished pictures. The results were spectacular and my daughter proudly displays the 18 x 18" colored portrait of her father. I subsequently used Le Deane Studios for many portraits of my kids. Found out a few weeks ago that he is still in business in Tucumcari!

The ODEON THEATRE

Tucumari (pop 7,000) sits along the 1-40conidor and old US Route 66 and is better known for its billboards that span for hundreds of miles either side of town , luring tired travelers with promises of numerous and comfortable accommodations, than it is for its recreational opportunity. However, visitors who spend more than just a traveling night in the Tucumari area will find the area is ripe with good fishing and wildlife viewing venues.

Lodging options in Tucumari are vast, with the town boasting over 1500 rooms, and travelers on all types of budgets will

find a dean room here. Dining in Tucumari ranges from fast
food to higher end steak & seafood restaurants and visitors
are sure to find something to please the palate here.

It's "Believe It Or Not" time. We had a movie theater. The Odeon. A
small storefront was wedged in between two larger buildings just off
Main Street. Movies were shown usually on the weekend and were
first run. Jim and I occasionally hired a baby sitter and went to see the
current offering. My clearest memory is of taking Ruthi to "Bambi"
and dissolving in tears right along with her in the middle of the movie.
I still get teary eyed when I think of the plot of that movie. Once a
month, the kids in town were offered the opportunity to earn free
tickets. They were given printed brochures that they distributed all
over town and won two free tickets to the theater. My two oldest were
enthusiastic participants.

A dance teacher suddenly appeared and advertised in the local paper.
Ruthi was the obvious candidate for lessons. She learned tap, classical,
swing and ballet. The man lasted about one and a half years, but Ruthi's
first career was to dance professionally from the time she was eighteen
on until she developed a tumor on her upper leg that, upon removal,
damaged some of the nerves and muscles in her leg. She still does a
mean "Salsa".

Another one of the church families were ranchers. I rarely did see the
father, but the mother brought the daughter to church regularly. They
had three boys who had a reputation for being rowdy. We were invited
to dinner one Sunday after church and had a lovely meal with the
family. After dinner, the boys said we were all going target shooting.
Well, who was I to refuse. I never had held anything more lethal than
a BB gun. Here I was with a 30 ought 6 and told to shoot at a can
a distance away. Feeling a little bit like Annie Oakley, I finally got
the strength and courage to pull the trigger. The resulting force of
the gun knocked me flat on my backside, knocked the wind out of
me and convinced me that I never wanted to touch a gun again. The
can . . . what can? I don't even remember looking to see if I had even
approached it with my shot.

The beautiful daughter was engaged at that time to a local boy who went joy riding on Route 66. He ended up driving full speed under the back of a semi truck. He and his friends were decapitated. Jim had to conduct not a wedding, but a funeral.

I mentioned earlier in my narrative about the bible burning which was fostered primarily by the John Birch Society. In Tucumcari, they were certainly Christian in their thinking, but way off to the right. Dan, Margie and their compadres were staunch members and they did wield some power in the decisions made by the community. Especially any efforts to change structure or protocol in the town. They were convinced that these were communist plots intended to enforce their twisted politics on all of us. Headlines in the local paper appeared one time in response to a building project to make downtown a Western town—MASTER PLAN FOR CITY DENOUNCED.

I am bringing up this family because they were central to a plan our family had come up with. Jim had read that the AFS (American Field Service) in Washington was encouraging people to take exchange students into their homes for a period of time that would allow them to complete their high school education. Our family all got together and chose a young man from Kenya, a member of the Kikuyu tribe who needed two more years to get his high school diploma. He would then proceed to medical school to become a physician like his older brother who now practiced in India. All the plans were made. Ricky, being our oldest boy, was eager to share his room and said "Will Simon be my older brother?" Simon was in a training session for two weeks headquartered in New York and would fly out on a particular day. We were to drive to Albuquerque to pick him up. Jim had consulted the superintendent of schools to see if there would be a problem, since Simon was obviously black. There were no objections. He had presented our plan to the session, Dan being clerk of session. There were no objections. So we happily proceeded. The night before Simon was to fly out, we were outraged by a phone call from Dan saying that the session had held a private meeting the night before and decided "no way were they going to allow a black man to be a part of our home or the church". Some of the statements were unreal . . . "we own the house you live in and no way would we let a black man live in their house with your wife and

64

daughter present". "Would you take a bath in the same tub as a black man?" Jim's answer to that was "probably I would leave a bigger ring in the tub." Well, we knew we were fighting an uphill battle and that Simon would be treated badly, so we called AFS. They cancelled our arrangements and quickly transferred Simon to Cazenovia, New York where we were able to maintain a correspondence with him for years. He did finish medical school, practiced in New York state until we lost touch with him. I "googled" him a few years ago, but only was able to contact his ex-wife who had had a bad experience with him. I just let it all go.

Jim had a theory that he called "pedestilarianism": The new pastor comes to the church and is placed high on a pedestal for all to respect. After awhile, someone takes an ax and starts to chip just a little from the pedestal. Then someone else comes along and picks up the ax and chips away. Finally the pedestal is gone and the pastor falls. This certainly is true of the political field as well.

The handwriting was on the wall and we knew it was time to prepare to leave Tucumcari.

—ᵐ—

Don't get sick in Tucumcari !!

We had only been in town for a month or so and were sitting on the front porch while the kids played in the street, a common practice as our street had very little traffic. We were eating fresh peaches when I suddenly became aware that my 18 month old son, Steve was choking on a peach pit. By the time I snatched him up to help him, he had swallowed it. With my nursing background, I knew that the throat is the smallest part of the alimentary canal so I was not so alarmed. But, since there were only two doctors in town and one of them was married to one of our staunchest members, I called his office to get advice. Dr. X came on the phone and said to feed the child two tablespoons of flour. My immediate response was "dry flour???" He said "Yes". I hung up the phone in disbelief because I knew that dry flour when placed near a nose or mouth is going to fly away. Good judgment made me realize that we could always check on "the daily output" to be sure it passed. And it did!! So much for my first medical encounter. Can you guess?? We never consulted him again.

During one summer, I was selected to be a counselor at our Presbyterian summer camp in the mountains above Taos. I was delighted and looked forward to our planning meeting being held at the campground. We decided to bring lunch and so I was carrying a basket of food in one hand and balancing all my papers and books in the other. I started down the slight incline to our picnic table, my feet rolled on some pebbles and I sat down with a thump, sliding down the balance of the hill on my backside. Well, where is America's Home Videos when you need them. We all had quite a laugh and went to our meeting. About a month after this, I woke up one morning and couldn't move my head. I felt like my head was stuck on top of my body to be immobile forever. A new chiropractor had come to town and Jim suggested I go see him, since we had no regular doctor in town that we were seeing. The first thing he did was take a full body x-ray. In order to see the brain stem, he asked me to open my mouth wide when he filmed me. When the film was developed, we met with him in the consulting room where he had posted the x-ray on the viewing screen. With x-rays, all solids are white. When Jim saw it, his comment was "That's Mary. I'd have known her anywhere. Her mouth is wide open and there is a blank space above". I loved his sense of humor. In fact he once complemented me on my "hour glass figure" but then said that the sand was running to the wrong end. My measurements . . . "a perfect 36—12 12 12."

A team of doctors finally arrived in town and set up a clinic. I had a serious sinus infection and so, rather than go all the way to Amarillo, I decided to go see them. The doctor who examined me was very thorough and said that he would "crack the turbinates" which are small outgrowths along the inside wall of the nasal passage. He said this would allow the sinuses to drain. In order for me not to be a screaming maniac due to pain, he said he would deaden the passage. In those days, cocaine sat in a glass jar on the counter, along with gauze pads, q-tips etc. etc. Well, he swabbed a q-tip up my nose. I proceeded to fall off the examining table and land on the floor, out like a light. I just don't understand the attraction of cocaine to the druggies of this day and age. I certainly would never willingly try it again.

An article I just read dealt with a new center for integrative medicine being opened in Albuquerque where modern, traditional Chinese, ayurvedic medicine from India and the Native American healing methods were being combined. Working with yoga instructors, doctors of Oriental medicine and hypnotherapists as well as certified medical personnel, the clinic is near the University of New Mexico campus and is being called "complementary medicine". The mestiza contributions were given by Hispanic curanderas. Sounds like a good idea to me. Incidentally, somewhat like witchcraft, it is still practiced to a great extent here in the Los Angeles area. I used to drive by a large Santaria candle factory in south L.A.

I had worked at Marin General Hospital while Jim was in seminary. During that time, we had experienced a polio epidemic but since I had survived what has been diagnosed as "polio", I was the technician who was sent in to do the lab work on polio patients in the isolation ward. Becauseof this, I took a great interest in the fact that polio immunization had come to Tucumcari. I volunteered and worked in the community center administering the vaccine to all the children and more vulnerable adults. The vaccine was dripped onto a sugar cube making it easy to swallow. New Mexico was getting settled into the 20th century!

Amarillo, though being far away, was our choice for medical care. It was a very large metropolitan city and we felt we would have choices. Also, it gave us a chance to enjoy some of the culture that was available. And who can deny the shopping!!! One of our care givers was a pediatric dentist. It came time for Ruthi (age 9) to have her teeth cleaned and checked so I asked my friend Clara if she wanted to go along. She was delighted to have the opportunity to leave her big batch of kids with neighbors for a day and have a nice trip. We started out in the morning with heavy winds, but no concern. We got as far as San Jon (pronounced San Hone), 15 miles into our trip and the sand was blowing so hard I had trouble seeing the road. Clara got out to walk ahead of the car until we got to a wider stretch of road, but that was impossible. This was Route 66, you know, and I was afraid I would run into cars ahead of me or get rear ended, but we were determined to go on. By the time we got to Amarillo, a number of hours later (usually a 2 hour trip at most), the blowing sand was gone but the winds were 50-60 mph. We saw the dentist and then headed downtown to have a luxurious lunch and do some shopping. The windows in the stores were bowing in and out with the gales and in some cases had shattered. I parked the car at the restaurant, we got out and a gale caught Ruthi and started blowing her down the sidewalk. Clara and I chased her, but the heel broke off of Clara's shoe and Ruthi finally was able to grab a meter and hang on until I could get to her and struggle back to the restaurant with her in tow. We had gotten the giggles and were collapsing with laughter by the time we finally got to eat. We went to the local department store and shopped until things settled down a bit before we headed home. The windshield and the whole front of the car remained pitted until we traded it in. An aside . . . I was pretty shocked to find that all the restrooms and water fountains in the department stores were segregated "WHITES ONLY". I had never seen anything like that before. This was early in the '60's!!

Ruthi's need for glasses at about ten years of age, became evident when we realized she could hardly see, but had successfully masqueraded the loss so that we didn't know. A trip to Amarillo was required. She had her eyes tested and we were told that she needed corrective lenses. When the exam was completed, she was ushered into a room to pick out her frames. They were all ensconced on the wall and she studied and studied, finally picking out one special one. She put them on and with a huge smile and squeal remarked "Oh, my, I can see so much better now!" We had to inform her that there was NO GLASS in the frames.

When the children were old enough to be in school full time, I took a part time nursing job with a new doctor who had arrived. Dr. P was married with children, but had grown up in Tucumcari so knew many of the townspeople. Gossip had it that he knew a lot of the women more than as just friends. One day, a lovely lady appeared complaining of a severe cough. I did a chest x-ray of her and put it up on the viewing box. She had pneumonia and Dr. P's comment was "D_____, I've been trying to get her to bed for a month". I hope the room was dark enough for him not to be able to see my face!!

He was an amazing diagnostician. One day, he walked down the hall, passed the bathroom, stopped and asked who was in there. I told him the man's name. He said "Check his blood sugar right away". Sure enough, the man was a diabetic and that explained all of the critical symptoms he was having. I asked Dr. P how he knew. He said he smelled it as he was walking by. Remarkable!!

One November day, we had just finished putting over 100 stitches into the head and torso of an 18 month old girl who had been attacked by their family's pet racoon. I fixed a cup of tea and was standing at the window with the radio on when the news came through that Kennedy had been assassinated. What a feeling of unreality. I'll bet everyone can remember where they were on that day.

One of our patients was a rancher who had caught his foot in a shredder. Dr. P had done extensive surgery. The man would come in every few days for us to remove the bandages and replace the cast. This particular day, Dr. P came in to look at the foot that I had x-rayed. I thought it had healed amazingly, but Dr. P said "I'm sorry to tell you this, but the foot will have to go". The man stared at him with alarm, his mouth dropped open and suddenly, he just sighed and laid back down. Dr. P picked up the cast cutter, turned on the noisy motor and started to cut . . . the cast. Cast cutters will not cut any soft tissue. Apparently, they were old school buddies and were always pulling mischief on each other. Lots of laughter of relief followed . . . and of course, a few four letter words.

Because I also did the lab work for the office, we always collected urine samples from new patients to do a complete study. Dr. P had requested a urine sample from an elderly man who did not speak much English. He was unable to provide a sample at the office so I instructed him with much pantomime, what to do when he got home and bring in the result. Imagine my amazement when the man appeared with his sample . . . in a pie tin.

One of the questions asked in our introductory questionnaire provided to the patients at their first visit was "Do you menstruate regularly?" One lady was very thorough in her response which read

"Yes, but only with my husband".

—⁂—

Our family had the privilege of six years in Tucumcari . . . wonderful memories that I am delighted to share in this story. Jim died August 31, 2001, just 10 days before 9/11 after almost twelve years of infirmity. He had served his country and was buried with honors at Riverside National Cemetery having earned the bronze star as a wounded combat medic. He fervently served as a pastor for 42 years and was a true servant of God. He served in Beverly Hills, Tucumcari, New Mexico, Wichita Falls, Texas, Michillinda Presbyterian Church, Pasadena, California (for 17 years) and went on after retirement to 7 years of interim ministry all over the nation. Many times during those years he would ponder the thought of whether he had ever really made an impact in peoples lives. After his death, letters poured in citing instances of "life altering" experiences people from all over had through his care and counseling. I read them all aloud for him. Many of the testimonies at his memorial service echoed this sentiment. An endearing moment at the memorial service was when our dear Rabbi friend's widow spoke of our times together in Europe. She ended her speech by saying "and we were the only Jews at their Christmas Parties".

As I am sitting in my car on a gridlocked "parking lot" freeway, gazing off toward the blurred San Gabriel Mountains, all of which I have climbed, and enjoying a smog inspired sunset, I often find myself longing for the quiet, simple life I led in New Mexico. Then I remember going to the Music Center to see Baryshnikov dance, hear the music of the Philharmonic, play with my grown up daughter at Disneyland, see my grandchildren reveling in the pleasure they have had at Knott's Berry Farm and I don't feel so bad.